EERIE EDMONTON

EERIE EDMONTON

RHONDA PARRISH
with RONA ANDERSON

DUNDURN
TORONTO

Publisher: Scott Fraser | Editor: Dominic Farrell
Cover designer: Sophie Paas-Lang
Cover image: goodfreephotos.com/WinterE229
Printer: Webcom, a division of Marquis Book Printing Inc.

Library and Archives Canada Cataloguing in Publication

Title: Eerie Edmonton / Rhonda Parrish, with Rona Anderson.
Names: Parrish, Rhonda, 1967- author. | Anderson, Rona, 1958- author.
Identifiers: Canadiana (print) 20190199539 | Canadiana (ebook) 20190199547 | ISBN 9781459744493
  (softcover) | ISBN 9781459744509 (PDF) | ISBN 9781459744516 (EPUB)
Subjects: LCSH: Ghosts—Alberta—Edmonton. | LCSH: Apparitions—Alberta—Edmonton. | LCSH: Haunted
  places—Alberta—Edmonton. | LCSH: Edmonton (Alta.)—History.
Classification: LCC BF1472.C3 P37 2020 | DDC 133.1097123/34—dc23

We acknowledge the support of the Canada Council for the Arts and the Ontario Arts Council for our publishing program. We also acknowledge the financial support of the Government of Ontario, through the Ontario Book Publishing Tax Credit and Ontario Creates, and the Government of Canada.

Printed and bound in Canada.

VISIT US AT

 dundurn.com | @dundurnpress | dundurnpress | dundurnpress

Dundurn
3 Church Street, Suite 500
Toronto, Ontario, Canada
M5E 1M2

Contents

Introduction 1

Rhonda's Story 4

About Rona 7

How This Is Going to Work 13

Part One: Public Spaces and Buildings

1   The Alberta Legislature — 9820 107 Street NW 17

2   Unnamed Restaurant — 10354 82 Avenue NW 26

3   Fort Edmonton — 7000 143 Street NW 30

4   Walterdale Theatre — 10322 83 Avenue NW 42

5   University of Alberta — 116 Street & 85 Avenue 56

6   Super Dougie's Ink — 6503 118 Avenue NW 65

7   Edmonton's Bluebeard 69

8   Felicia Graham 73

9   Westmount Junior High School — 11124 130 Street NW..... 79

10 Charles Camsell Hospital — 12804 114 Avenue NW 83

11 Dominion Hotel Building — 10324 82 Avenue NW 103

12 The Guilty Martini — 10338 81 Avenue 108

13 Garneau Theatre — 8712 109 Street NW 115

14 Wee Book Inn — 10310 82 Avenue NW 120

15 Mount Pleasant Cemetery — 5420 106 Street NW 124

16 Edmonton Cemetery — 11820 107 Avenue NW 128

17 The Granite Club — 8620 107 Street NW 132

18   Edmonton 1881 School — 10425 99 Avenue 135
19   Alberta Block (Former CKUA Building) —
     10526 Jasper Avenue 139
20   Scona Pool — 10450 72 Avenue NW 144
21   Queen Elizabeth School — 9425 132 Avenue NW 159
22   Masonic Order Freemasons Hall of Edmonton —
     10318 100 Avenue NW 163
23   Strathcona Museum, Sherwood Park — 913 Ash Street,
     Sherwood Park 166

Part Two: Private Residences

24   Private Residences: A Different Approach 175
25   Brittney — Knottwood Area (Millwoods) 177
26   Chloe — Central Edmonton 180
27   Janice — Kilkenny 182
28   Corinne — Glenora 184
29   Daryl — McKernan 187
30   Cassandra — River Valley 190
31   Premee — Alberta Hospital Edmonton 193
32   Sandi — Devon 195
33   Fraser — Gateway Boulevard 205
34   Mike — Castle Downs and Gariepy 208
35   Tanya — Parkallen 212
36   Ghost Cats 219

     In Conclusion 222
     Acknowledgements 224
     Sources and Further Reading 227
     Image Credits 231

Introduction

According to the *Oxford Dictionary*, the word *haunted* describes a place "frequented by a ghost." This can include outdoor areas, buildings, and houses. Books on the paranormal usually focus on the United States, the United Kingdom, and Europe. The histories and guidebooks related to these places, some of which have existed for hundreds of years, also often recount tales of ghosts and other spooky sightings.

You might be surprised to learn that a young city like Edmonton also has a cache of haunted and spooky places. Although the city is only 127 years old, Edmonton actually has a rich and fascinating history, which includes the Klondike Gold Rush and exploits of fur traders, and history-rich locales, such as Fort Edmonton. And, adding to that, a really wild, wild west persona. Of course, the land on which Edmonton is now located was, for thousands of years, the home of Indigenous Peoples.

Edmonton was incorporated as a town in 1892, with a population of 700, and then as a city in 1904, with a population of 8,350. Pretty small pickings. Edmonton became the capital of Alberta when the province was formed a year later, on September 1, 1905. Today, the city has a population of almost one million.

So you think, "How could Edmonton have a bunch of haunted places?" Well, as I said, people have lived on the land that Edmonton stands on for thousands of years. It's not surprising that some of their spirits — the ghosts of the sad, the angry, the deranged, and even those who just wish to remain in the place they liked during their lives — should linger on. And of course, there are the spirits of those who died violent deaths: those killed in the many battles over land between settlers and Indigenous Peoples; those who lost their lives in the wars between Indigenous Peoples; those who succumbed in the innumerable fights between settlers, transients, and fur traders. The Gold Rush itself claimed thousands of human lives because of starvation, freezing temperatures, and exposure to the elements. That leaves a lot of dead people.

Now, not everyone who dies decides to haunt an area or building, but Edmonton is home to its fair share of spirits who decided to stay for one reason or another. There are some areas of Edmonton that are more haunted than others, and a couple of areas have very negative energies attached to them.

Parts of the northeast side of Edmonton and some neighbourhoods in the central west end have spooky vibes and have experienced lots of crime and violence in the past. Iconic, historic Strathcona in Edmonton is a big tourist and shopping area. It has a plethora of buildings on and off Whyte Avenue — also known as 82 Avenue — that are haunted. The Westmount area contains some haunted buildings, and there are many in downtown Edmonton, with the ever-changing Jasper Avenue.

Edmontonians love Halloween and really go crazy every year. The city has at least twelve pop-up Halloween stores every year, and hundreds of homes attract huge numbers of people who come to see the latest scary Halloween home fronts. There are large haunted amusements, such as Fort Edmonton Spooktacular, Rutherford House (both of them), and Deadmonton Haunted House. As well, at least thirty other major events take place in October. The city also has a hearse club, the Edmonton Bone-Wagon Association, which consists of several hearses. And many cosplay, witch, and metaphysical markets and events take place all year round. So, you can see Edmonton is a very otherworldly place.

The one bothersome thing about Edmonton and its connection to haunted places is the extreme reluctance shown by Edmonton Tourism, as well as building and business owners, to promote the fact that the city has haunted places. Edmonton has haunted pubs, restaurants, and rooms, but no one advertises any of it. Hopefully, one day in the future, Edmonton will embrace its paranormal hotspots and include them in the city's tourism and promotional advertising.

Just an FYI: This book is collaboration between Rhonda Parrish and me — she is a writer who specializes in adventurous subjects and themes, and I am a paranormal investigator and psychic medium who communicates with earthbound spirits. We went into as many areas and structures as we could, and I related to her who or what I saw that inhabited them from the spirit world. Some places we could not get into because of various reasons, so I related to her past events I had seen and experienced. Other places we were told about by residents of Edmonton, as places to check out.

Note: We are not responsible for spirits who might have left buildings or taken possession of establishments during the time this book was written and published.

— Rona Anderson

Rhonda's Story

"Tell our server they should unlock that stall door because they are getting a lurker spirit in there."

Rona said that while she and I were in PUB 1905 — we met there from time to time to work on this book, because I am positively addicted to their poutine. Rona was referring to one stall in the women's washroom that is perpetually locked. I assumed it was out of order, but, to be honest, I hadn't given it much thought until Rona told me a lurker spirit was hanging out in there.

Earlier that afternoon, we'd been talking with the server about ghosts and eerie happenings, so I knew she was receptive to the idea of spirits. That didn't mean, though, that she was necessarily going to be super excited about the idea that one had taken to hanging out in the washroom where she worked. And since Rona was on her way out the door when she asked me to pass the message on, I got to be the bearer of the bad news. All by myself.

When the server came back to the table, I said, "So ... I feel like an explanation is required here. People learn and discover new things about our world all the time, so I believe that anything is possible, but I'm pretty skeptical when it comes to the paranormal. I tend to think that if something unusual happens, the most likely explanation is a mundane one. My friend, on the other hand, is very much a believer. In fact, she can see and communicate with ghosts."

The server nodded and I continued, "And she asked me to tell you that you should unlock that stall door in the washroom because, with no people going in, a lurker spirit has started hanging out in there."

The server took it in stride. She barely even blinked. I suspect that's because she had a ghost story of her own already. Because if writing paranormal nonfiction has taught me one thing, it is this: everyone has a ghost story. Even us skeptics.

Here's mine:

I was four or five years old when it happened. We were living in a red-brick house in Nanton, Alberta. I really liked that house — the tree out back was great for climbing; my brother and I got the whole upstairs of the house to ourselves; and, best of all, the window upstairs opened up right over a section of the ground floor's roof so we could play out there, too … as long as Mom didn't catch us.

There were no hallways upstairs; it was just two big rooms, separated by a wall running half the width of the house. There wasn't a door in that wall, just a big opening that served as a portal. The stairs from the first floor delivered you into my brother's half of the attic — his room — and my room was on the other side of the wall.

Late one night, when I was creeping back to my room after going to the bathroom, I saw something I couldn't explain.

The house was quiet but for my light tread on the rather creaky stairs, and dark. The only illumination came from the streetlight shining in through the window in my room, and most of that was blocked by the wall. My brother was sleeping in the far corner of his room. As I climbed the stairs, I could hear his soft breathing and see his vague outline in his bed.

That was as it should be.

The man standing at the very top of the stairs — between me and my brother, and also between me and my bed — was not as it should be.

He shouldn't have been there.

No one should have been there.

Looking at him, I realized I wasn't sure he *was* there.

The shape of a man was there — tall, thin, wearing a hat, maybe — but it was more like a shadow within a shadow than a physical form. Sort of like a different shade or quality of darkness.

You know how when you close your eyes tightly in a bright room, so it's dark but not completely dark because shadows, after-images, and specks of light are playing over the inside of your eyelids? He looked like that. Like he was made up of static, after-images, and weird light.

I paused just before the top of the stairs.

I wasn't scared. I wasn't not scared. I think I was mostly confused.

And then he was gone.

He didn't vanish in a flash, or fade away like smoke. He was just gone.

There one moment, gone the next.

Or was he?

I've always had a pretty active imagination. And this did happen late at night when I was, at best, half-asleep. Was it some sort of waking dream?

Questions. So many questions.

Maybe that's part of why I wanted to write this book with Rona. Because, in addition to a lot of great stories, she just might have some answers.

About Rona

Rona doesn't remember a time when she couldn't see ghosts. According to her mother, when Rona was about three years old, she began talking to someone named Glick. No one else could see Glick, but apparently he was a full-grown man. Rona would have very in-depth conversations with him. Conversations that would be far too complicated for a three-year-old to come up with all by herself. Based on that fact, and the abilities that Rona eventually developed, she and her mother believe that was the first spirit she ever spoke to.

Although there were a few unexplainable encounters after that, when Rona would see things no one else did, the first otherworldly encounters she strongly remembers took place several years later, when she was nine or ten years old and living in Gimli, Manitoba.

The first happened when she was babysitting her little sister. She could hear someone jumping on her parents' bed. Her first thought was that it must be her little sister, but no … her sister was in the bedroom they shared, playing quietly with Barbies. Rona ran into her parents' bedroom to see what was going on. There was no one there, but the bed was all mussed up, as though someone had been playing on it. Confused, but not wanting to get in trouble for messing up her parents' bed, Rona made the bed and went to hang out with her sister, hoping no one would notice that anything was amiss.

Some days after the near encounter in her parents' bedroom, things became a bit more personal. As Rona and her sister were trying to go to sleep, the closet door kept opening by itself. Imagine being nine or ten years old and having a closet door that just keeps opening up by itself. Spooky! And things were about to get even worse.

The bedroom Rona shared with her sister had roller blinds — the kind of blind that allows a person inside a room to see shadows of what's on the other side. Rona kept seeing the shadow of a man holding an axe, walking by the window. As most children would, she freaked out and kept yelling that a man with an axe was coming, but when her parents investigated, there was no man. No axe. Nothing. Thinking they were dealing with a child with an overactive imagination, her parents would just say, "Be quiet and go back to bed."

But Rona had seen his shadow. She knew she had.

Rona's parents got divorced when she was eleven, and then she and her sister moved with their mother to Barrie, Ontario. That was when things got even scarier. And much more personal.

"That house was *haunted*," Rona told me over a plate of poutine at PUB 1905 while "Live and Let Die" blasted from the speakers. "And I think it was haunted because I was there. Because I think the people who were haunting it were my aunt and uncle."

That aunt and uncle had died suddenly and violently. Frequently, at night, Rona would hear the distinctive "swish, swish" sound of a woman walking up and down the hallway in her nightgown. Even though she wasn't able to see the spirit, Rona knew, without question, that it was her aunt. After pacing back and forth for some time — time that felt especially drawn out to the young girl cowering beneath her blankets in bed — her aunt would stop outside Rona's bedroom and jiggle the handle of the door. One night, after enduring weeks of this, Rona steeled herself and summoned up all her courage.

When her aunt stopped to jiggle the door handle, Rona ran to the door and flung it open.

Nothing was there.

Although she never saw her uncle's spirit in that house, Rona knows he was there, too. She thinks he hid from her because he was really ashamed of what he'd done in life and how he'd died.

In addition to her aunt and uncle's spirits, a third, darker spirit also inhabited the house. This third spirit, which Rona describes as "not nice and not quite human," lived in the basement. There was a storage room in the basement, which everyone called the cold room because it was always colder than the rest of the house. "Whenever I had to go into the cold room to get [something], the hair on the back of my neck would go up and I knew there was something in that room." Rona says sometimes "weird" spirits can attach to people who have committed suicide, and she believes that one of these spirits became attached to her uncle and was inhabiting the cold room.

"I know a lot of people say, 'Oh, it was a demon,' but it's not a demon," she said when I asked her if these spirits are sort of like shadows attached to the spirits of some suicides. "It's some other human spirit that's really a lot darker than what he was."

The family dog wouldn't even go near the basement, let alone the cold room. She would whine and cry and stand with her tail tucked between her legs anytime anyone tried to make her go downstairs.

Unfortunately for the kids, that was where they spent most of their time — it was a place where they could be out of the way of the grown-ups. Rona recalled, "We had to be in the basement with the bad stuff … if I had been older and understood what happens with spirits, like the way spirits are, I wouldn't have had any fear, but back then I didn't know enough, I wasn't educated enough."

It sounds like the plot of a horror movie, doesn't it? Relegate the psychic kid and her little sister to the basement with all the ghosts.

Not only did Rona see and sense spirits at home, but she also encountered them outside. One day, Rona was playing at her friend Joanne's house and she looked out the window and said, "Hey, your mom's here."

The problem was that Joanne's mother had died several years before.

Joanne got very upset and began crying, and Rona was sent home.

Rona laughed, telling the story now, but one can only imagine how difficult it was for her as a child to see these things and not be able to tell anyone about them; to have to carry all that weight on her own.

But Rona did learn from these encounters. The next time she saw Joanne's mother, while she and Joanne were playing in her basement, she didn't tell the other girl.

The scariest thing that happened in Rona's house occurred when she was seventeen. A dark, malevolent spirit visited her in her bedroom. Rona was suddenly woken from a sound sleep. Her room was dark, but she sensed there was something in the corner of the room; something even darker than dark. It was a seven-foot-tall male shadow that radiated menace. Rona knew in an instant that he was completely negative and she didn't want anything to do with him. Terrified, she closed her eyes tight and willed him to leave. Thankfully, he did.

These days, Rona knows how to handle spirits, but even when she was younger, she had learned that not all ghostly encounters are scary. When she was nineteen, she was lying in bed and saw an electric-blue toddler filled with stars. There were so many he couldn't contain them; they surrounded him like a nebula.

"Mom," he said, coming up to her bed. "Mom, I had a nightmare."

Rona said, "Okay, I'll tuck you in. Don't worry about it."

And then he dissolved into nothing as if he wasn't even there.

Some days later, she was woken up by something invisible jumping onto her bed. She could feel it move on the bed, its weight disturbing the mattress beneath her, and then it settled up against her and began to purr.

These, Rona told me, were "foretellings." The little boy in blue turned out to be her son. One night, years later, that exact scene replayed, with him waking her up because he had had a nightmare and they had exactly the same conversation; the cat also came to her in its physical form some time later. And when he did, Rona's heart recognized him, even though she'd never actually seen him before.

When Rona was about twenty, the paranormal part of her life really began to grow and take over. "It was, like, now I'm seeing spirits, now I'm feeling spirits, now I'm hearing them."

I asked her how she was able to figure out what she saw and sensed. She told me that it took a lot of time — it's not as if there's a class you can take that will explain all this — but eventually she realized she was seeing the spirits of people who were troubled and didn't know where to go, or who knew where to go but didn't want to go there. She calls these earthbound spirits.

Most psychics, she says, communicate with loved ones who have died, but that is not something she is able to do. As you'll see throughout the rest of this book, Rona can communicate only with spirits before they have passed over to the other side (with very few personal exceptions). What does that mean, you ask? Well, it means she can communicate only with spirits who are trapped here, in the reality that you and I also inhabit. Once spirits have moved on to an afterlife, whatever form that takes, she no longer has the ability to sense or speak with them. So, for example, she can't do readings for other people, but she can go into a building and see the ghosts that are haunting it.

In her late twenties, Rona started to do paranormal investigations with her partner, Ben. They met like-minded people online, and eventually they all met up in person to formalize their group and acquire some equipment. Now, although Rona does investigations and clears locations — releasing the spirits so they can move into the light — she doesn't bother to bring the equipment to most sites. She is able to help people without all the bells and whistles. And helping is her main goal. "I want these people to be at peace when I leave," she told me. "I don't want them to be fearful anymore."

The whole time we were talking, I could see a gentleman at the table next to us, alternating between leaning closer to try to hear what we were saying and rolling his eyes so hard I was worried he would hurt something. After he left, I asked Rona if that happened to her a lot — if she constantly had to deal with people being jerks to her because of what she believed. Basically, she shrugged it off.

When I asked her, as someone who comes to all this from a very skeptical place, how she addresses people's skepticism (in our case, I made a conscious decision to accept that *she* believes everything she tells me, even if I might not believe it all myself), she said, "Even if they are skeptical, I can [tell by looking in their eyes] that they either know somebody who has experienced something or something happened to them that they're not sure about … but I don't want to get into an argument. I'm not trying to change people's minds. I'm just saying this is what I see."

That she didn't simply shrug off people's skepticism made me happy, because it convinced me that the road we were going to travel over the course of working on this book would be relatively smooth. I would respect her position even if I couldn't adopt it for my own, and she, in turn, would respect mine even if it didn't match her reality.

That was the only way this could work, really.

How This Is Going to Work

I'm going to share dozens of spooky and paranormal stories set in and around Edmonton. Some of these stories describe events in places Rona and I visited together, some will be my recounting investigations Rona performed before we ever met, and some will come from other people. I have worked hard to avoid "everybody knows" and "friend of a friend of a friend" stories and have attempted to stick with first- and second-hand tales.

Before I even started writing this book, Rona and I had several conversations about how it should be done — what the rules should be.

Establishing the rules for the interactions between me and her was quite easy. We knew it was entirely likely that if Rona and I were to experience a potential paranormal phenomenon, we would interpret it in two completely different ways, but we'd respect each other's interpretations even if we didn't subscribe to them. Perhaps more importantly, I made a very conscious decision to accept that Rona believed everything she told me. Again, I might not subscribe to the same philosophies, but I can respect that Rona does. So, I have reported everything Rona told me as fact.

That was how things worked between us — mutual respect and open communication.

Further, I extended that same respect to everyone who shared a ghost story with me. Even though I am skeptical when it comes to the paranormal, I don't think it's any fun to try to rip people's stories

EERIE EDMONTON

apart, or try to prove that their experiences are mundane rather than supernatural. That was not my job here. My job was to record, as faithfully as I could, what they told me; to compare it, whenever possible, with the verifiable history of the haunted location, and look for any connections between them.

I'm not looking to play spoiler, but I feel like it's important to state my skeptical bias right up front. I did this when talking to people whose experiences I'm passing on, but I'm also doing so with you, the reader.

But what about the haunted locations and finding connections between the ghost stories and their verifiable histories? How did that work?

Well, in an ideal world, Rona would never have visited any of them; nor would she have known any of the history. If that were always the case, we could have applied something resembling scientific method to our research and investigations. Unfortunately, we do not live in a perfect world.

People who are interested in the paranormal tend to seek out ghost stories and ghostly encounters. And people like Rona, who make that interest more than just a passing hobby, seek these out even more. So, before we started, Rona had quite a lot of knowledge about the sites in Edmonton associated with the paranormal. To complicate things even further, Rona is also a bit of a local history buff, so she knew some of the history of these locations even before we hit up the city archives. So, no: sadly, there were very few blank slates to be had before we broke ground on this book.

With that in mind, I've taken care to share how familiar Rona and I were with each location. I begin each section with a discussion of the verifiable history of the place, then recount what we knew going into each location. After that, I go over the paranormal encounters we had there or that we could find stories about, and finally I end by trying to make connections, if possible, between the paranormal events experienced in each locale and the known history of the place, to see what conclusions can be drawn.

Buckle up. It's going to be quite a ride.

PART ONE:
PUBLIC SPACES AND BUILDINGS

- 1 -

The Alberta Legislature — 9820 107 Street NW

History

The Alberta Legislature building was built between 1907 and 1913. It has a symmetrical T-shape, with a large central dome above a rotunda. All the windows and doors have beautiful arches or lintels, and the very front of the building includes a portico held up by massive columns.

The Leg (pronounced *ledge*) overlooks the North Saskatchewan River and is surrounded by expansive, beautifully landscaped grounds. When it was first constructed, however, it loomed over the original location of Fort Edmonton. There are a great many photographs showing the fort in the foreground and the Legislature building behind — a contrast of tradition and progress.

I love the way Paula Simons described it in a story she wrote for the *Edmonton Journal* on October 23, 2015, where she said:

> It's a physical testament to the courage and of the people who forged this province. And, if we're honest, of their arrogance, too.

The Alberta Legislature building and grounds.

Built on the original site of Fort Edmonton, where aboriginals and Europeans traded, construction began in 1907, when the population of Edmonton was less than 15,000. Imagine the colonial hubris to construct such a magnificent sandstone palace in the midst of the frontier. Imagine the surreal absurdity of imposing this quintessential classical European form on the wild banks of the North Saskatchewan River. *

Unfortunately, this beautiful building has been the site of two separate shootings — the first in 1977 and the second, eleven years later, in 1988. Interestingly, neither of them was politically motivated.

---

* edmontonjournal.com/news/politics/paula-simons-albertas-legislature-reopens-its-front-doors

On October 27, 1977, Guenter Hummel entered Cabinet Minister Horst Schmid's office, carrying a long gun. There he shot and killed Schmid's secretary, Victoria Breitkreuz, and then turned the gun on himself. Guenter and Victoria had been in a romantic relationship and had even lived together for a time before Victoria broke things off.

The second shooting occurred on October 14, 1988, when Robert Crawford, a man angry about his child custody arrangement after a bitter divorce, attempted suicide-by-cop. That morning Robert showed up at the Alberta Legislature with a .30-30 rifle. According to an *Edmonton Journal* article, again by Paula Simons,* the first person Crawford encountered was Commissionaire Herb Bushkowsky, who, upon seeing Crawford loading his gun, asked, "Do you have a problem?"

Crawford replied, "Several."

At that point, Bushkowsky locked the door and called 911.

For several hours after that, Crawford wandered the grounds. He didn't engage bystanders; in fact, he warned them away, but kept trying to provoke security and police into shooting him. Eventually, he found another way into the Legislature building and into the Leg's beautifully marbled rotunda.

The police confronted him there and, despite the officers' best attempts to defuse the situation, a shootout occurred, during which Crawford was injured.

Having been in that space and heard how much it echoes just with the normal day-to-day activities of politicians and tourists, I can only imagine how it must have rung with the sound of the bullets during that shootout, when at least seven shots were fired. It would have been loud enough to wake the dead, as my grandmother might have said.

Later, at Crawford's trial, it was revealed that he had taped notes to his arms saying he refused all medical treatment and that he wanted to die. He did not die. Crawford survived, although he was

---

* edmontonjournal.com/news/local-news/the-day-an-angry-gunman-attacked-alberta-legislature-26-years-later-the-story-of-robert-crawford-has-horrid-echoes

left unable to walk and was later reported to have complained that he had counted on the police to "be better marksmen."

There are still two bullet holes in the elevator doors in that main rotunda as a result of the shootout.

What We Knew Going In

Rona and I were both familiar with the Leg, because of course we were. It's the seat of our provincial government, a regular site for events, and a popular destination for families throughout the year (and especially in the summer). Neither of us was especially familiar with its history, however. When we visited, it was the first time Rona had ever been inside the main building. It was my second visit, but the first had lasted only a few moments.

Encounters

The rotunda of the Legislature building is beautiful, bustling, and super echoey. Everything is marble, the space is wide open, and there is a white-noise machine masquerading as a fountain right in the very centre of it all.

When we arrived, it was relatively empty — only a small family, the people who worked there, and Rona and I were loitering in the area.

Rona thought she could sense a male spirit upstairs; unfortunately, it was on a level that was off limits to the unaccompanied public. I suggested we could ask if the free tour would go up there, but Rona figured being part of a tour would make it difficult to pick up on anything. Instead, I left her on a bench on the periphery of the room where she could see the spot, and so as not to interfere with her picking up any ghosties that were about, I went to the other side of the room and wandered around.

I looked back over at Rona frequently. I won't lie, I was hoping to see some outward sign of her peering through the veil, but alas, there was nothing. No trance; no rocking back and forth. Not even a single eye-roll. Basically, she just sat on the bench, looking up at the upper level opposite.

I left her alone until I saw that a tour guide had approached her and they were chatting. Thinking that meant her ghost-watching time was done, I crossed the marble floor and joined them.

I wish I'd made note of the guide's name, because she was lovely. She breezily accepted that we didn't want to be part of the tour that was going to start in a few minutes, but in an effort to help us out, because we were obviously very interested in the building, she offered us passes that would allow us to go into the library and archives in the back, where it would be quiet and there would be books. Old books. I love old books, and I thought the quiet of the library might also be conducive to Rona sensing some more spirits, so of course we said yes.

I thought it was probably a good omen that my badge number was 187, because one-eight-seven has long been used as a synonym for murder (on account of Section 187 being the criminal code number for that crime in many places), and murder and ghosts seemed like things that would go hand in hand.

Unfortunately, although there were a lot of interesting things in the library and archives room (including a cheeseburger encased in resin), Rona didn't sense any spirits back there. She did, however, manage to get a fix on the spirit she'd sensed back in the noisy rotunda. There were two of them, in fact.

By the time we came back out into the rotunda, the guided tour was about to begin, so the place was packed with people and their voices echoed around the room, creating a cacophony of noise. I was disinclined to linger.

Once we'd turned in our badges and were standing on the front steps of the Leg, I asked Rona to tell me what she'd seen so we could capture it while it was still fresh in her mind.

The first spirit she had sensed was that of a man, up on the second floor overlooking the rotunda. He was a handsome and stylish man, with dark hair and a dark suit. "He was a lawyer," Rona said. "I don't know if he was a lawyer who went into politics or if he was just a lawyer." He seemed happy and was enjoying watching everyone come and

Looking up in the rotunda in the Alberta Legislature building. Rona spotted two spirits up on the third-floor hallway.

go in the rotunda — the bustle and excitement of a day at the Alberta Legislative grounds. Rona described him as a very, very positive spirit.

The second spirit Rona encountered also seemed to be quite positive — she was a woman in her midforties, proudly pushing a

Another look at the upper levels of the Alberta Legislature building and the main domed ceiling. Is it any wonder the acoustics are remarkable in this cavernous chamber?

cleaning cart. She was plump, with short, curly brown hair, and a rounded nose. She was very proud of herself for continuing to do her job and keeping the Leg clean even after her death.

"She was in a pretty good mood for someone who cleans," Rona quipped. "Because I've cleaned before." She shook her head in a way that made it clear it had not been her most favourite job ever. Then she returned to talking about the spirit.

"She's Polish, and her name either began with *N* or ended with *N* — or maybe it was her nickname? People called her Nan. I don't know if she was like a grandma; maybe that was why she was called Nan?"

I looked for more stories of ghosts or hauntings at the Legislature, without much luck. All I turned up were a lot of stories about political ghosts (usually in reference to politicians losing power in one way or another), and one dark photo that purported to show a ghostly figure in a window of the West Wing. Unfortunately, no matter how hard I squinted at that picture, I couldn't see anything out of the ordinary. Alas.

But when I posted on Facebook, asking if anyone had any Edmonton ghost stories to share, Val L. Bate stepped forward. Val used to work as a security guard in the Legislature building. She said that whenever she had been in the front area, she felt uncomfortable, and that the gold elevator there would frequently open and close all by itself. Every shift, she said, you could count on the gold elevator's doors to open and close without anyone around to have pushed the button.

That elevator, it should be noted, just so happens to have two bullet holes in it.

Connecting the Dots

Unfortunately, I don't think there are any dots to connect here. I have no reason to believe that any of the two people recorded as having died in the Alberta Legislature building are haunting it — unless, perhaps, one of them likes to play with the elevator. But the prevailing belief about ghosts is that they aren't bound to the place of their death, anyway. If you subscribe to that theory, the spirits Rona sensed may have died somewhere else and then come to the Leg after their deaths.

Tracking down the spirits Rona saw would, I think, be nearly impossible. A dark-haired male lawyer in a nice suit. How many hundreds of them do you think have come and gone through the Leg in the hundred-plus years of its existence? As for Nan, to begin tracking her down, we'd have to uncover what company (or companies) have been contracted to clean the building in the past few decades — Rona was able to identify that the cleaning cart and supplies looked relatively modern, which means we wouldn't need to go back the full hundred years — and then, by some miracle, get access to their employee records. Then we'd need another miracle to be able to identify Nan from those, because all we have is that nickname and the fact she was Polish. All in all, there's just not enough to go on.

- 2 -

Unnamed Restaurant — 10354 82 Avenue NW

History

This location has been the site of many businesses since the building was first erected. It is also the site of paranormal energy. Rona believes this derives from a time when it was a family home.

I made a few phone calls, most notably to the Provincial Archives of Alberta and the Alberta Land Titles Office, to find out how I could learn if this address had ever been registered as a private residence rather than as a business. I discovered I would first have to acquire the legal address rather than the municipal one, which is actually rather simple. But then I would need to go through all the historical title transfers and check them individually to see if that location had ever been home to, well, a home. That wouldn't necessarily be too bad — except for the fact that each individual title search costs money. It's a small amount of money, ten dollars each, but it wouldn't take too long to add up. And because I have no idea how far back I'd have to search … I decided that whether this location had ever officially been zoned as a private residence might just have to remain a mystery.

What We Knew Going In

Rona and her partner, Ben, had investigated this location twice back in about 2010, so she was familiar with it. She had never actively done any research on its history, but she had heard rumours that it might once have included a residence of some sort. I had absolutely no knowledge of or experience with this location in either a paranormal or mundane capacity.

Encounters

This particular location has been home to several different restaurants. Unfortunately, Rona is unable to recall the name it was known by when she visited, which is why I'm calling it the "Unnamed Restaurant" for this chapter. It's not because it doesn't have a name; it's because we're not sure which one it was using at the time. We do know that the restaurant was just opening and there was a news story about it, in which one of the staff members happened to mention she believed there was a ghost there. Intrigued, Rona and Ben approached the restaurant and asked if they could investigate.

At the time, there was a fireplace in the restaurant and the staff set up Rona and Ben at a table near it. Sitting at the table, surrounded by oblivious diners and wait staff, Rona watched as a man with tremendous anger and his wife relived an intense domestic violence scene. While people ate their dinner and chatted happily, these two, dressed in clothes from the late 1800s, yelled and screamed and *fought*.

"What that restaurant had," Rona told me, "was residual energy."

Residual energy is different from an intelligent haunting. It's more like an imprint that has been left behind from something traumatic. Analogies used to explain residual energy usually focus on fingerprints (same idea: something that was there leaves a mark that's usually invisible to most of us), but I prefer to think of it like the indentations heavy furniture leaves in carpet. Once the furniture is gone, you can still see where it was. With some work, if you have the right tools and know-how, you can remove those marks and no one needs to know the furniture was ever there, but if you don't actively do something, the marks will linger and everyone who enters that room will know exactly where your bookshelves were. So, it's kind of the same idea … but with energy.

According to the theory, when a traumatic event plays out in a space, it leaves a psychic mark, and people who are sensitive to these sorts of things experience the residual energy through a change in temperature, or of mood. People who are extremely sensitive or psychic, like Rona, might actually watch the scene play out. Sometimes over and over, like a movie on an eternal loop. Unlike with an intelligent haunting, residual energy is unchanging and will not respond to people around it.

Rona believes that this location, which is now a restaurant, probably included a residence at some point, and that this scene, or something very much like it, played out there often between this couple. The good news is that it's not an intelligent haunting — this woman is not trapped in an endless cycle of suffering and abuse. The bad news is that their lingering energy could affect the moods of people who come across them.

This location also boasts an intelligent haunting. At the time of Rona's visit, the washrooms were located down a hallway; she'd heard that many people, when going down that hall, reported feeling like something was wrong, without being able to put their finger on exactly what. When Rona went down the hallway, she couldn't pick up on a particular spirit, but she believes that was because the spirit recognized she would be able to see it, and it went into hiding while she was there. Most likely, Rona believes, this happened because the spirit sensed she had the ability to move it over to the other side and it didn't want to leave. It was having a good time here in our reality and didn't know what might be waiting for it should it pass over.

Connecting the Dots

Because we don't know whether there was ever a private residence at this address, it is impossible to know the likelihood of Rona's theory that the domestic violence scene she'd witnessed was a re-enactment of something that had happened over and over again at a time in the distant past, when that building was a house rather than a business. However, even if we had that information, it would be very difficult to verify, especially as, even in modern times, domestic violence is often under-reported.

As for the intelligent haunting, it's interesting that Rona felt it was actively hiding from her, because that suggests a degree of insight into Rona and self-awareness of itself that not every spirit seems to have. However, if it was going to hide every time Rona came near, that does, by extension, make it very difficult to learn more about it.

I think any connections between the residual energy and the spirit near the back washrooms and this location's history will have to remain a mystery for now. Perhaps someday, Rona will be able to sneak up on the shy spirit and learn more about it. Never say never.

- 3 -

Fort Edmonton — 7000 143 Street NW

What We Knew Going In

Rona had visited and investigated Fort Edmonton on a couple of occasions and was quite familiar with its history even before we began working on this book. I visit the park almost every year to soak up the atmosphere and take a lot of photographs — mostly of horses and chickens. There isn't a blank slate to be had for this one, but there are several really interesting stories just the same.

Fort Edmonton is broken into four general areas and time periods:

- 1846 Fort, representing 1795–1859, the fur trading era
- 1885 Street, representing 1871–1891, the settlement or homesteading era
- 1905 Street, representing 1892–1914, the municipal era
- 1920 Street and Midway, representing 1914–1929, the metropolitan era

Visitors can enter and walk around in several buildings in each of those, and often there are also costumed interpreters who are happy

Dozens of orbs loiter outside the historic church at Fort Edmonton Park.

One of many flying orbs spotted among some of the heritage buildings at Fort Edmonton Park.

to answer questions and provide information while in character as historical figures. All in all, it seems like a very welcoming environment for spirits from days gone by.

The Original Rutherford House

History

Although many of the buildings at Fort Edmonton Park are reproductions, Rutherford House is an original structure. Once the home of Alberta's first premier and the founder of the University of Alberta, Alexander Cameron Rutherford, in 1968 it was moved from its original location of 87 Avenue and 104 Street to the park. Once in place on 1905 Street at Fort Edmonton Park, the house was rejuvenated by the City of Edmonton Artifacts Centre and Fort Edmonton Park, based on all the information at their disposal, including archival photographs.

This house was the home of Alexander Rutherford and his family from 1895 to 1911, when they moved into a new home on Saskatchewan Drive (on the present-day University of Alberta campus). Mr. Rutherford served as the premier of Alberta from 1905 to 1910, when he stepped down after being implicated in the Great Waterways Railway scandal. This means that the entirety of the time he served as Alberta's premier, he called this, the original Rutherford House, his home.

Encounters

When it came time to visit Rutherford House at Fort Edmonton, Rona showed up before everyone else in her group, hoping to scout the house before the rest arrived. The door at the front entrance is an old one — you have to lift the latch and then push it in to open it. Rona entered, latching the door closed behind her, and went up the stairs to explore. Just as she got halfway up the stairs, she heard the sound of the latch lifting and turned around to see the door ajar. Rushing down the steps, Rona looked outside to see who was there. She saw no one.

"There was no human around who opened that door from the outside," Rona said. "And for somebody to open the door, [the latch] needs to be … lifted up and pushed … so that latch has to come up."

In other words, the door couldn't possibly have opened itself.

On another night, when Rona was there with a group of friends, she saw smoke coming out of the chimney. But there was no fire in the chimney. Perhaps the spirits were chilly?

And there *are* spirits. Later on, over the course of her investigation, Rona met some of them. An interesting trio of them, in fact.

The spirits inhabiting this house are not the people who lived there in life. "It's almost like," Rona said, "you leave your house and squatters come in. That's what it's like."

These squatter spirits have good taste; I can think of much worse places to call home in the afterlife.

There are two ghosts haunting it full time, and one who stops by to visit now and then. The first is an older Scottish gentleman. He has a full beard and moustache that are starting to grey. He has a great sense of humour and is very fond of his pipe. When he moved in, he claimed the master bedroom as his own, he informed Rona, because the bed in that room reminded him of his bed back in Scotland. He spends most of his time walking around upstairs, smoking his pipe and — who knows — possibly pondering the mystery of the universe (because why should that stop just because one's heart has?). His name, according to what he told Rona, is Mr. Jameson.

Down one flight of stairs from the master bedroom is a small bedroom that was taken over by a spirit Rona refers to as a scullery maid, for lack of a better description. This young lady looks to be from the early 1900s — somewhere around 1910, Rona guesses. The spirit has a slight build and brown hair, and she is very shy. She wouldn't speak to Rona at all; she just kept going about her business, fulfilling her domestic duties: tidying, cooking, that sort of thing. She would sometimes hide if the other spirits came into her area of the house. Rona got the impression that her name was Milly.

A third spirit, a young man in a First World War uniform, shows up regularly to visit with Milly. He doesn't stay at the house like the other two spirits do, but comes by to see the ghostly girl he is smitten with. The only name Rona got for him was "Towser," which is obviously a nickname. She couldn't get a handle on his full name.

He is younger, in his early twenties, like Milly. He has what Rona describes as a lopsided smile and a dimple in one cheek.

These three spirits have created their own sort of family in the afterlife. The maid looks after the Scottish gentleman, who in turn feels protective of her and wants to be sure the soldier's intentions toward her are good. It's really quite charming. Almost like a ghostly version of *Downton Abbey*.

Some time after her initial visit, Rona also visited the house accompanied by a CTV crew, which included a cameraman, a soundman, and reporter Carolyn Jarvis, who has beautiful, long red hair. They were standing in Rutherford House and Ms. Jarvis was interviewing Rona about it.

"Do you sense anything here?" Carolyn asked.

Rona said yes, and told her about the Scottish man, the maid, and the soldier. She explained which parts of the house the man and the maid usually occupy; she also mentioned that Mr. Jameson had come out of his room and was with them.

"He's telling me," Rona told the reporter, "that he likes women with red hair and he really wants to touch your hair."

Ms. Jarvis was not a big fan of that idea. Rona remembers her looking quite distressed and saying something like, "Oh, no! What? No!"

Rona, who deals with ghosts all the time and has a rather big mischievous streak, thought that was pretty funny and decided to play it up a bit.

"You know what? All he wants to do is go like this," Rona said and mimed a soft stroking action.

Ms. Jarvis did not like that. In fact, she said she wanted to leave the room and the ghost's presence. However, as they were leaving,

Mr. Jameson's ghost, who has a mischievous streak himself, followed along. He was laughing and said to Rona, "Oh, but I just want to touch the back of her hair."

In the end, Rona convinced him not to touch her, because it's one thing to tease someone about something like that; quite another to touch them when they don't want to be touched. Rona doesn't mess around with crossing that line. Even with ghosts.

Connecting the Dots

Unfortunately, I have no idea how to begin trying to link the paranormal activity that Rona experienced in Rutherford House and the property's history. The spiritual squatters were never associated with the house during their lifetimes, and Rona can't remember seeing a regimental number or any other identifying feature on the soldier's uniform, so we haven't really got any real information that we can use to identify them.

In a way, it's almost too bad the Scottish gentleman told Rona he was going to touch Carolyn Jarvis's hair. If he had just done it — if he had touched her — there would be something tangible to report on, and another skeptic might have experienced something they couldn't explain. As it is, we just don't have enough information to figure out who these spirits are or if, despite what they told Rona, they are connected to the house in any way. If you ever visit Rutherford House at Fort Edmonton Park, however, Rona definitely suggests calling Mr. Jameson to see if he'll come by. But she does warn that if you have red hair, he may give it a little pull.

Firkins House

History

Construction on the Firkins House,* a Californian bungalow-style building, started in late 1911 and was completed in mid-1912, which was when the house's first owners, the Firkinses (originally from the United States),

---

* fortedmontonpark.ca/1905-street/the-firkins-house-a-profile

took possession of it. At that time, it was located on a secluded part of Saskatchewan Drive, overlooking the river valley.

Dr. Ashley Martin Firkins and his family lived in the home for some time while Dr. Firkins practised dentistry in Edmonton. During the time they lived there, two daughters, Carolyn Roberts Firkins (September 12, 1911) and Miriam Roberts Firkins (November 2, 1912), were added to their family.

Sometime before 1933, the family sold the home and moved. Later, Dr. Firkins died in Compton, California, on March 10, 1933, when the building that housed his dentistry practice collapsed in a 6.4-magnitude earthquake.*

In 1992, after Firkins House had gone through several other homeowners, the Karpetz family donated it to Fort Edmonton Park. The house's Edwardian architecture and its stucco on the exterior, which was quite new for Edmonton at the time of its construction, made it a wonderful addition to 1905 Street.

Encounters

A bloody bathroom. A traumatized family. So many questions. Rona doesn't know the details, but she can sense the residual energy from the event. "There was a very violent accident. I'm not sure what happened, but somebody smashed their head on either the sink or the bathtub.... I do believe it was the sink," Rona told me. "Something happened to them and they fell and hit their head on the sink. And it was very upsetting to the whole family."

The good news is that whoever the injured person was, Rona and her spirit guides feel sure they survived.

A very quick note about Rona's spirit guides, because they are occasionally a source of information for her, like they were at the Firkins House. Rona has at least three of them, who communicate with her through something that sounds a lot like intuition to me, but louder, easier to hear and understand. We won't get into detail about them, because that is a subject for another book, but often when Rona

---

* findagrave.com/memorial/71398165/blanche-carolyn-firkins

tells me she is given to understand something, or has been told something, the information is coming from one of her spirit guides.

Right. So, back to Firkins House. In addition to the residual energy from the accident in the bathroom, Rona says there is the spirit of a little boy.

"[Some people] say 'Oh, it's the ghost of the boy who died there,' but it's not. There was no little boy who died there," Rona said, disdain evident in her voice. She's confident that the spirit of a boy haunts the property, but it's possible he's come from somewhere else, like the ghosts that are currently occupying Rutherford House. Unfortunately, Rona never got a good look at him, but she definitely sensed him there and believes he has a red ball he likes to play with.

The rumour about the spirit of the boy who is said to have died at Firkins House probably originates from the defunct television show *Creepy Canada* (season 2, episode 3). In that show, the producers tell a story about someone who, while volunteering to stay the night in the house as part of a radio station's Halloween event, saw a boy who appeared and then vanished without explanation. In that same episode of *Creepy Canada*, there is also a story about a ventriloquist's dummy that is able to move around the house under its own power and belonged to a boy who died in the house. In that story, the doll was the lonely boy's only friend, and it continues to haunt the house even after his death. According to that same television show, when a woman tried to redecorate the boy's bedroom, she was physically attacked by his spirit.

I wanted to mention the *Creepy Canada* episode because it *does* recount a ghost story about this location, but I don't want to retell its stories in detail because I find them a little problematic. They seem a bit too Hollywood and they are exceptionally vague. No names are given for the boy or his family, for example, and everything is a re-enactment; there is no original footage and there are no photographs or witness interviews. And I'm not the only one who finds it troubling. In an interview for *Avenue Magazine*, Kevin Spaans, who played Ashley Firkins at the park for a long time, said of the *Creepy Canada* story, "It's all bullshit."

For this book, I'm trying to stick with first- and second-hand sources, so I don't want to repeat stories that are of the "legends say …" variety. Those can certainly be a lot of fun around a campfire, but it was not the direction I wanted to take with this book.

So. Enough about that television show's ghost stories, and back to Rona's (it's possible Mr. Spaans would also dislike hers, but at least a name is attached to it).

Back in the mid-2000s — 2004 or 2005 — Rona was one of the subjects of a news story in the *Edmonton Journal*. As part of the story, a reporter and a photographer went with Rona and some of her colleagues to Fort Edmonton Park. The journalists started out very skeptical, but while they were in the children's bedroom in Firkins House, the photographer started to frown. "Well, that's not right," he said, looking at the display screen on his camera.

"What's not right?" Rona asked.

"There's something wrong with my camera," he said.

But when Rona looked at the screen, she knew nothing was wrong with his camera. He'd just captured the image of a ghost on it.

"There was this form coming up from the floor. And it was purple."

Rona was very excited about the spirit he had captured on camera; the photographer, however, was far less enthusiastic. In fact, after inspecting his camera and discovering nothing wrong with it, he began to become a bit freaked out. So, too, was the reporter. In fact, they were upset enough that when they left Firkins House and Rona suggested going down the street to where they would find more spirits, the pair decided they didn't want to continue.

They went from supernatural skeptics to believing enough to be unnerved and just wanting to go, all after one visit to Firkins House. That's pretty powerful.

Other stories persist about this house. I found several websites claiming that while the house was being constructed or renovated, tools would be mysteriously moved or go missing altogether. And people also claim to have seen a mysterious woman floating through the house; others have said they found doors that were impossible to open, and smelled phantom scents.* Unfortunately, I was unable to find any first-hand accounts of these stories, only retellings of retellings.

Connecting the Dots

It seems that Rona was correct when she said no boy died in the house; in fact, the Firkins family didn't even include a young boy. It is possible that one of the families who lived in the home after the Firkinses had a son, but there is no way I'm going through all the property records and family histories to find out — in part because if one believes in ghosts, then one has to make allowances for squatter ghosts. According to Rona, Rutherford House has a few squatter spirits, so it's possible that Firkins House does as well. Perhaps there's one who takes the shape of a little boy. However, I'm going to go out on a limb and say that it's *really* unlikely a boy ever spent his dying days in that house, learning to do magic and possess a doll that continues to haunt the property.

As to the question of doors that can't be opened, the Fort Edmonton Park website explains that they didn't remodel the upstairs bathroom, so that door remains permanently locked. Is that the mysterious unopenable door? I can't say for sure because I couldn't find any primary sources that specify which door could not be opened, but it definitely seems possible.

On the same note, I found it interesting that aside from Rona's recounting, I wasn't able to find a single first-hand account of a haunting at Firkins House, despite the fact it is frequently touted as one of the most haunted locations in Edmonton. Further, according to an article by Omar Mouallem in *Avenue Magazine*,** none of the employees of Fort Edmonton Park, including the ones who dress up as Dr. Firkins and his wife (and thus spend many hours every day in the house), have ever reported a single supernatural occurrence. In fact, Mr. Mouallem leaves us with the wonderful image of the

---

* cambridge.org/elt/messages/infoquest/ghosttours/sites/firkins/page5.asp

** avenueedmonton.com/October-2009/The-Firkins-Ghost-Buster

interpreters, "sitting on the porch of the old Firkins home sipping tea, nibbling cucumber sandwiches, discussing Edwardian poetry with ardent loquacity and quashing every supernatural inquiry like Whac-A-Mole."

One Night During an Eclipse

One night, which just happened to be the same night as a lunar eclipse, Rona and Ben were hired as guides for a haunted ghost tours–type adventure. Basically, the organizer had rented a bus and driver and sold tickets to a bunch of women who were looking for some ghostly fun. They drove around the city while Ben and Rona pointed out some of the most interesting ghostly hot spots and shared some of the stories and history of the locations. The cherry on top of that haunted sundae was meant to be Fort Edmonton Park. The organizer who had rented the bus had also paid for them to take it into the park for a short time — Rona thinks they were given about an hour.

Their first stop was Firkins House, where Rona spent a good amount of time dispelling rumours that a boy had died on the premises, and then she shared her own supernatural experiences at the location. After that, they went to Rutherford House. They had been allowed to move around freely in the Firkins residence, but at Rutherford House they were confined to the living room. "So," Rona told me with a laugh, "we looked around the living room." They admired the furnishings and the fireplace, which was non-functional at the time, and after hearing Rona's stories about the place, they left and loaded back into the bus.

As the tour participants got back on the bus, they were looking out the windows, at the eclipse. Ben happened to look back at Firkins House and noticed a light on in one of the bedrooms. "Hey," he said. "I turned that light out before we left, but now it's back on."

The house had been locked up behind them, so they couldn't just go back in to turn the light off (or see what was happening in the house); they had to go get someone who worked at the park to unlock the door and turn it off. So they did. They went and found the young woman who'd been tasked with, basically, supervising their time at the park, and had her come back to turn the light off. She was not happy about it; she was scared of going back into the house by herself to turn the light off. Ben offered to go with her, so she wouldn't have to do it alone, and together they went back in, turned the light out, and locked the door behind them once more.

Then Rona looked over at Rutherford House and made another surprising discovery. Despite the fact that the fireplace in the house was non-functional, there was smoke coming out of the chimney.

At that point, Rona says, the poor girl who worked for Fort Edmonton looked at it and said, "Nuh-uh. I am not doing anything about that."

Instead, she went to go get security to look into the situation and make sure nothing was awry.

Unfortunately, Rona was on the clock to return the bus and had to leave before she could find out how that event resolved — whether security spotted anything odd in the house or not.

It should be noted that there is no reason to think these events were tied to the lunar eclipse in any way; it's just a fun coincidence that they happened at the same time.

- 4 -

Walterdale Theatre — 10322 83 Avenue NW

History

Walterdale Theatre is housed in a former fire hall, one of the oldest major fire halls in Alberta and the last remaining pre–First World War fire hall in Edmonton.* Built between 1909 and 1910, it is a beautiful red-brick structure with round arches over a trio of double vehicle doors and a brick bell tower. Originally called the Strathcona Fire Hall No. 1, it existed to serve the city of Strathcona, and when Strathcona and Edmonton were amalgamated in 1912, it was renamed Edmonton Fire Hall No. 6. It continued to function as a fire hall for more than four decades, but in 1954 a newer, spiffier fire hall was built and this one was decommissioned and became storage for a furniture company. In 1974, however, it was renovated and started a new phase of life as the home of the Walterdale Theatre.

It underwent another major renovation in 1992 to expand its seating capacity. In fact, it seems that over the years, the building has undergone several renovations, some more extensive than others.

---

* hermis.alberta.ca/ARHP/Details.aspx?DeptID=1&ObjectID=4665-0681

Walterdale Theatre is housed in an old fire hall, originally built in 1910.

I haven't been able to connect any specific firefighter deaths in Edmonton to the fire hall that eventually became Walterdale Theatre. Most firefighter deaths I could find information about were related to post-traumatic stress disorder or diseases that were likely contracted or exacerbated by things they came into contact with on the job. According to a 2017 *Edmonton Journal* article,* only twenty-nine firefighters have died in the line of duty since 1922, the most recent of which was in 1976. So, while it is possible there was a firefighter death associated with the Strathcona Fire Hall No. 1 or Edmonton Fire Hall No. 6, at this point I can't confirm or deny that.

What We Knew Going In

Rumours abound about Walterdale Theatre being haunted, and Rona was aware of the stories before she went in. As for myself, I'd attended a show there before but hadn't heard about or experienced any specific paranormal stories related to it.

Encounters

The ghost stories surrounding Walterdale Theatre are numerous, but vague. They include accounts of phantom smells of horses, the unexplained ringing of the bell, and a feeling of being watched.

In 2015 Eric Rice, Walterdale Theatre's president, told the *Edmonton Journal,* "Our own stories are ambiguous. [People have reported] feelings of someone in the building, lights coming on unexpectedly, sounds of someone else in the building."**

There are reports of people encountering the spirit of a firefighter they call Walt, or Walter. In the *Journal* article, Walt is described as being "oddly dressed" and is frequently blamed for (or credited with) moving things around and creating breezes; some have claimed that he will occasionally assist people who are climbing the stairs.

---

* edmontonjournal.com/news/local-news/firefighters-lost-to-occupational-disease-in-spotlight-at-edmonton-fire-rescue-911-memorial

** edmontonjournal.com/news/local-news/we-see-dead-people-10-spooky-edmonton-haunts-in-which-you-might-find-some-halloween-spirit

Ben and Rona were invited to investigate the theatre because people believed there was a spirit there and wanted to know more about him. Who was he? What did he want? Unfortunately, at the time of their investigation, there was a play in production and the company didn't want the paranormal investigators there for very long, as they could disrupt the preparations for the show. Still, even in the short time they were there, Rona was able to pick up on a spirit in the theatre. He didn't specifically identify himself as Walt, but I'm going to call him by that name because that's what the other people who believe in him have called him.

Walt, according to Rona, is a mischievous spirit. Rona said she and Ben "kinda guessed that he was [a] firefighter who died from smoke inhalation many, many years ago." Further, they got the impression he was impatient for them to leave so he could "get down to his dastardly duties of playing with the makeup and moving stuff."

Rona believes that, at least in part, people can sense there is a presence near them at Walterdale Theatre but can't actually put their finger on where it is, because Walt is very active, always bustling about, pulling pranks or just overseeing the goings-on at the old fire hall.

Rona believes that the other unexplained events people have reported experiencing in the building — the phantom ringing bell and the smell of horses — are the products of residual energy remaining in the building, rather than intelligent haunting.

"[It's not that there are] spirits of … horses … stuck there; it's just that they [did] their job over and over and over again for such a long time that it left an imprint in that dimensional place, and something will trigger it and you'll hear the horses clopping and the bell going off. I don't know what the trigger is."

Possibly, if she'd had more time in the theatre and there had been less hustle and bustle, Rona would have been able to pinpoint the trigger or discover more details about Walt, but unfortunately that wasn't how it worked out.

Happily, I was able to meet with Geri Dittrich, who is a costume designer for Walterdale Theatre. She and I met up at the theatre early in the morning, before anyone else was there, and she gave me a tour and we talked about her ghostly experiences.

I liked Geri immediately. She struck me as someone who is very efficient in everything she does, but who also puts a lot of heart into it. No nonsense, but warm just the same.

She and I have similar levels of belief in the paranormal, so it was easy to find common ground. I explained that I'm skeptical about the paranormal. "I believe that anything is possible. I don't *not* believe," I said. "But I think most things have a mundane explanation."

"I'm the same way. I believe in energy," Geri said, speaking words I'd heard come out of my own mouth more than once. Then she went on, "And I do believe in a presence. But I believe it's a personal thing, and I really shudder when I see people come in with gadgets, because I don't think that's it. I think it's a state of mind and where you are.... So, a lot of it can be explained, but a lot of it can't. We like to think there is a presence here."

In talking with Geri, it became very apparent that for a lot of people, the theatre is like a second home, containing a second family. And perhaps a ghost as well. The attitude around the theatre seems to be one of inclusion, an "everyone is welcome" sort of feeling. In fact, when I sent Geri and Joan (a set designer at the theatre, whom I also interviewed about Walterdale) the stories I'd written up after speaking to them, just to make sure everything was factually correct, they each, separately, responded to say that yes, everything was as they'd described; however, they preferred to refer to the theatre as Walterdale, not *the* Walterdale, because, as Geri explained, "We tend to think of the place/institution/society as a living entity, a buddy, an old friend, a patriarch." So, it does not surprise me at all that this community would welcome and embrace a ghost.

As Geri showed me around, I discovered that the building itself is unique: not only because it used to be a fire hall, but for lots of other reasons. For one thing, a handful of little hidey holes and back passages is sprinkled throughout it — the better to get actors, unseen, from one spot to another. There are no *Phantom of the Opera*-like secret passages into the sewers — at least none that I know about — but there are a few places someone could hide to pull pranks.

Space is at a premium at Walterdale, and none of it is wasted. There are things tucked into every corner, and every space can be used for more than one purpose: storage, rehearsals, you name it. During its more active hours, I imagine it must practically hum with energy, but when I was there, early in the morning with only Geri and I in the building, it was a quiet place, despite the fact that there were plenty of echoes. Very peaceful, and kind of cozy. Which is an odd way to describe a building with so many large rooms, but accurate just the same.

Sound is unusual in the theatre. There is a magic spot onstage where you can hear what is going on in almost all the different parts of the theatre. On the other hand, the supply room is so stuffed full of costumes and awesome miscellanea that it acts like a huge sound-proofing chamber — if you're standing at the door, someone just ten feet inside might not be able to hear you.

I love the supply room. It's my favourite space in the whole build-ing. When I was younger, we lived in a drafty old house, and my room had a walk-in closet. Inside the closet were one or two things shrouded in dry-cleaning bags and a lot of wire hangers. I used to sit in that closet, listening to the soft murmur the hangers made as they moved against each other in the air currents. It felt like they were talking, and if I only listened hard enough, I would be able to under-stand them. The supply room at Walterdale Theatre had that same sort of feeling. As if it shares a border with something magical, and if I spent enough time in there I would hear the stories the clothes and hats and shoes had to tell.

"I've never seen the ghost in here, though," Geri said as we were leaving the supply room. "He doesn't dare."

"No?" I said, watching Geri put back some hats that had slid out of place. "Because he might knock things down?"

"Because he might not get out," she said with a laugh.

The supply room is upstairs, just across the hallway from the room containing Geri's fabric stash, and the sewing machines. She told me that sometimes when she needs more space, they pull all her equipment out into the room at the end of the hall, but it sounds like she does most of her work in the sewing room. It's one of the places she's heard the ghost. He wasn't in the room with her, but rather walking around outside it.

Actually, in all of the stories I heard about Walter, the ghost is upstairs.

Or on stairs.

There is a no-frills wooden staircase with worn green carpet tucked behind the stage, which leads right upstairs to the green room. It's definitely not fancy. It's also not very well lit, but despite that (and despite the fact that it would presumably be even less well lit during a production), I felt safe and secure as we walked up it.

Some years ago, the theatre was performing a period piece. No one seems able to remember exactly what the play was, but the general consensus is that it was set in the 1920s, or thereabouts. During one of the rehearsals, Frank — one of the actors — was the last person to leave the green room to go downstairs to the backstage. On his way down, he passed a young man in costume going up the other way. Frank didn't recognize the actor, but oftentimes during rehearsals, people practise in groups and he knew that it was possible they had no scenes together and his group just hadn't interacted with this other fella's. It was also possible that the younger man was an extra who had just been brought in that evening.

Anyway, Frank did his performance. For some reason, though, he was still wondering about the man in costume.

When he came back upstairs, he asked the people in the green room, "Who was that young man who came up the stairs? I haven't seen him around before."

The stagehands looked at him askance and said, "No one came up the stairs."

But Frank knew he had passed someone. Someone who seemed as solid and real as he himself was. And he knew that once you start coming up the stairs, there is nowhere to go but the green room. Or the bell tower.

"So *his* ghost was another actor he met in the stairwell who wasn't part of the show and nobody else saw him," Geri told me, making it clear what she meant when she said that spirits are very personal. She seems to believe that each person will experience the same ghost in a different way. I really like that idea.

The story of the ghost in the back staircase is one I heard more than once while researching the theatre. However, all my reports of it are second-hand because, unfortunately, Frank recently passed away, so I was unable to talk to him about it. The story lives on, however, and every time someone from the theatre shared it with me, I could hear a fondness in their voice. For Frank, and also for the ghost.

The bell tower is the only place other than the green room that the young man Frank passed on the stairs could have gone to. Looking up at it, Geri and I joked that the view from up there might be spectacular, but the climb to reach it didn't look very fun. Someone makes that climb regularly, though, because the bell that still resides up there is rung a few minutes before each show begins. Interestingly, because of the way sound works in the building, you can't actually hear the bell ringing in the green room, but people outside on the street can.

Geri told me she's never heard the bell ring when she didn't expect it to, nor had she heard first-hand of anyone else who has, either. She also hasn't ever heard the phantom horses.

Funny story about the wall between the main building and what used to be the stable, though. When Geri and I were walking through on our grand tour, she realized something. The brick arch on one side of the wall is set at a completely different angle from the arch on the other side of the wall. Looking closely, I could see there is a double wall there. I have no idea what the purpose of that would be — soundproofing?

weatherproofing? aesthetics? — but it's interesting to me for one reason above and beyond that. I love the fact that even though Geri has spent hour upon hour in that building, it still has the power to surprise her, even if Walter doesn't, necessarily.

Whenever Geri talks about Walter, she does so calmly, matter-of-factly. She speaks of him the way one might a flesh and blood acquaintance. It's really nice, actually.

Geri's most dramatic encounter with Walter took place, as so many of these encounters do, during renovations. The building had been gutted and so the theatre company had been forced to move over to the old Varscona Theatre to perform the shows left in the season. They were able to move back while they were working on the last show of the season. Some of the walls were still missing, there was still framing work to do, but the building was usable once more.

Geri had set up to work in what is now the rehearsal hall, and she was alone in the building. The rooms all around her were dark — the only light was coming from her workspace. As she was sewing away, she could feel something. She looked up. Nothing seemed amiss, so she returned to her work. But she could still feel something, as though she wasn't alone.

Geri paused in her work and turned around. There, with the big arched windows at her back, in the partially unfinished upstairs section, she saw a glow in the area that would later become the green room. There was no logical reason for a glow to be there. "It was kind of like an aura, but it wasn't round. It was sort of up and down with a bit of a bulge," Geri said. "Like a misty sort of thing." A glow that, Geri said, was much closer to a human shape than simply an amorphous blob.

And yet, the sight of that glow, which disappeared shortly after it appeared, didn't disturb her. It felt natural. Natural enough that her reaction to seeing it was just to put her head down and get back to work sewing the costumes. Only when she was done working for the night and had left the building did it occur to her that the glow might be something worth more than just a passing notice. It was as she was driving home that she paused and thought, "Oh, wait a minute. Did I just see a ghost?"

Retelling the story to me, Geri said, "I felt a presence. I didn't feel a shiver, or a cold draft or anything else."

Thinking back, Geri said there was no unusual light coming in through the windows; nothing reflecting. She even looked around the next day, trying to see if she could find a mundane explanation for what she'd seen, but she couldn't.

Geri continued to work on shows at the theatre off and on for many years without any further sightings, even though she often worked through the night rather than drive back and forth to her home in the country. It wasn't until several years later that she encountered Walter again.

By that time, the earlier renovations had been completed, and the upstairs of the theatre was fully functional once more. Geri wasn't working in the rehearsal hall, but rather the sewing room. She always kept the sewing room door propped open while she was in there, but because of the way the room was set up, she was sort of tucked behind the door as she worked. It obscured her from the view of people in the hallway, and also blocked her view of the hallway.

It was one o'clock in the morning. The theatre was supposed to be empty. Geri was still there, however, burning the midnight oil to make sure all the costumes were ready to go. Tucked away in her sewing room, Geri heard someone's heavy footsteps. "[The steps sounded like those of] a man on a mission." Great, stomping footsteps that began somewhere near her door, which is close to the top of the stairs, and step, step, stepping down the hall and into the green room at the end of it.

Curious about who it might be — she had thought she was alone in the building — Geri stopped working and moved to stand in her open doorway to find out. Her thinking was that perhaps it was someone who'd forgotten something and would be coming back with it in a moment. Passing her was the only possible way for them to leave, after all, because the door to the back stairwell (the only other way back downstairs) was locked. But no one came by.

In the days and weeks after that, it happened again. And then again. And again.

Geri would be working in the sewing room, thinking she was the only one in the building, and she would hear a sound like someone wearing workboots, or army boots. "It was a hard step. And it was a steady step," Geri said. It was a step she heard often enough that it became familiar — much like how you or I can identify the step of those we are closest to.

Similarly to after she saw the glow, it took her a while to wonder if the phantom footsteps ought to have warranted a bigger reaction from her. Then she heard other people talking about them.

One day, when she was talking to their technical director, Richard, he just straight up said, "Yes, there is a ghost here." And when Geri asked him why he could say that with so much confidence, he said it was because he could hear the footsteps.

It turned out that sometimes when he was working late at night, assuming he was alone in the building, he would hear a man's heavy tread walking around outside his booth. In the green room. The exact same space where Geri often heard the footsteps.

Like Geri, Richard didn't mind that they were sharing a space with the ghost. He didn't cause any mischief and made a handy scapegoat whenever one of the humans associated with the theatre misplaced things.

Some years after that, they were in the early parts of a production and were doing "cue to cue," which, Geri explained to me, is the technical check when they are setting lights and sound levels and timing things. They aren't practising the whole show but, as the name suggests, just going from cue to cue and skipping the bits in between.

The stage manager and operators were in the booth, and the directors and designers were downstairs with the cast. Geri, one of her assistants, and a couple of other people were sitting upstairs in the far corner of the green room. Knowing it was important to be quiet so that the stage managers could hear everything going on, no one was talking. They were reading books, or the script, or whatever. The point is that they were being very still and quiet, when suddenly the director, who was usually a very calm and easygoing man, stomped up the stairs and shouted at them to be quiet and quit walking back and forth across the floor. And then he stomped back downstairs, leaving Geri and everyone else upstairs very confused.

Once they got a break, they approached the director and explained that they hadn't been moving across the floor; they hadn't even been talking to one another. He didn't believe them.

So, while upstairs they hadn't heard anything at all, downstairs it sounded like they had been stomping around … in the exact same area where Geri and Richard had both heard the ghostly footsteps before.

As Geri and I were wrapping up our chat for the day, we were joined by Joan, who does set design for the theatre. She had a

The back exit of Walterdale sets an eerie mood, the perfect atmosphere for sharing ghost stories.

familiar-sounding story about hearing heavy-booted footsteps, which didn't seem to have a mundane origin. But what struck me most about her story was the fact she was disappointed she hadn't had a more profound experience with the ghost. She said that sometimes when she is working alone, she will pause and consciously open herself up, hoping for Walter to make an appearance, but other than the footsteps, he never has. "What am I?" Joan said. "Chopped liver?"

I empathize with her completely. Although I'm skeptical, now that I'm an adult I would very much welcome an experience that I couldn't explain. A ghostly encounter. But apparently I, too, am chopped liver.

Connecting the Dots

This building has undergone several rounds of renovations, and Rona says that renos tend to stir up whatever latent spirits might be about. Could that be the reason so many people have reported feeling as though there is a presence in the theatre, without being able to put their finger on why they felt that way? It seems possible to me.

Walt or Walter's name obviously comes from the name of the theatre he's said to haunt — *Walter*dale Theatre — and the fact he is spoken of so affectionately by everyone I talked to means it doesn't even matter to them what his history is, or how "real" he is. They love him regardless.

The heavy stomping footsteps that several people have reported definitely suggest that he might be the spirit of a firefighter, and just because I wasn't able to associate any firefighter deaths with the theatre doesn't mean he's not a firefighter. It could be that the footsteps are residual energy from years and years of firefighters treading the same path. Or it could be that a firefighter who died elsewhere has come back to spend his eternity at the fire hall because it was his second home. Or it might be that they are somehow caused by the weird acoustics throughout the theatre. Personally, I doubt the latter.

Given how attached breathing people are to the theatre, I don't find it difficult to imagine that a spirit would have the same attachment —

whether it be a firefighter or a former player (actors can stomp too, right?).

What about the person in period clothes who passed Richard on the stairs when he was going from the green room to the stage? The one who disappeared before entering the green room?

It's possible that he was a real person in period clothing and not a ghost, but if he was, the only place other than the green room that he could have gone to was the bell tower. And given that no one saw him at any point after the show, he would have had to stay up in the bell tower until everyone else had left, and then gone back downstairs to leave the theatre. Which is more likely? That someone dressed in period clothes went from backstage, up the stairs, all the way to the bell tower, stayed there alone for several hours, and then sneaked back down, or that Richard passed a spirit on the stairs? Keep in mind that the theatre wasn't robbed or vandalized or anything that evening, so there are no obvious motives for such actions.

Skeptical as I am, I'm leaning toward the spirit.

I have to admit, too, that the affection with which everyone talked about Walter — as if he were a beloved uncle everyone adored — has definitely biased me toward pulling for there being a ghost here at Walterdale. I can't help it. Everyone obviously loves him so much; I really want him to *be*.

- 5 -

University of Alberta — 116 Street & 85 Avenue

The University of Alberta campus is rather extensive, with many different buildings and areas. To best tell its story, I'm going to break it up into several smaller subsections.

What We Knew Going In

My husband works at the University of Alberta, so I spend more than an average amount of time on campus visiting him, attending events, and occasionally just taking photographs. I also wrote about Pembina Hall purportedly being haunted for the book *Haunted Hospitals: Eerie Tales About Hospitals, Sanatoriums, and Other Institutions.*

Rona had been to Rutherford House on the University of Alberta campus and picked up on a few spirits inside it, but she was not familiar with its whole history.

The Second Rutherford House: 11153 Saskatchewan Drive NW

History

This was the second house occupied by Alexander Rutherford and his family. He purchased the lot on which this house stands on May 29, 1909, and by the end of the year, the firm of Arthur G. Wilson and D. Easton Herrald had drawn up the plans for the home. The foundation was poured by the end of May 1910.

Alexander Rutherford; his wife, Mattie; and children, Cecil and Hazel, moved out of the house that was eventually donated to Fort Edmonton Park and into this, their new home, in 1911. Initially, they called the home Achnacarry, after their ancestral Scottish castle. They lived there for nearly thirty years, until Mattie died of cancer in September of 1940. After her death, in June 1941, Alexander sold the house to the Delta Upsilon fraternity for about as much as it had originally cost him to build it. Alexander subsequently died of a heart attack in hospital, less than a year after his wife died.

The Delta Upsilon fraternity occupied the house until 1969, when they were forced to leave because the University of Alberta had expropriated the land. The university's original intention had been to demolish the house to make room for expansion, but it was saved from that fate by a huge public outcry and preservation campaign. As a result of that campaign, the university began to lease the house to the Alberta government in 1970.

It was formally recognized as a historical location on June 28, 1979.

The house is currently a museum; it boasts a restaurant and offers guided tours, costumed historical interpreters, and special events. It also contains many artifacts from Alexander Rutherford and his family, which were donated by the family after his passing.

Encounters

Ben and Rona have hosted a Halloween ghost tour event at Rutherford House three times. On each of those occasions, they had an elaborate tech set-up, which included cameras — both normal and infrared — that captured significant amounts of spirit activity inside and outside the house. The most intriguing activity involved the spirit of a little boy.

Rona doesn't know why he was there — whether he was actually associated with the house or if he'd just come over from somewhere else — but he was very familiar with the setting and loved to run around. He looked to be somewhere between six and eight, had light hair, and was wearing brown cotton pants, brown shoes, and a plain shirt. At various times, Rona encountered him chasing a ball, or playing hide-and-seek. Always on the go, never sitting still — just like so many living boys I've known.

One time, Rona went down into the kitchen to talk with the staff before the event began. When she asked them if they had ever experienced something at Rutherford House that they couldn't explain, she got more than she could have anticipated.

I've been with Rona when she's asked this question, and the answer is almost always "yes" (which is part of the reason I say that everyone has a ghost story), but in this case, the story came with a photograph.

One of the worker's friends had been to the house to visit and had taken a photograph that showed the little boy, slightly blurred, as though caught in the middle of movement, running about the house. We have been actively trying to track these people down to share their photograph because Rona tells me that the boy in the picture looked exactly like the one she'd sensed in the building.

Further, some of the staff in the kitchen had also had encounters with the boy. They weren't afraid of him because he seemed to be mostly curious, not malicious. Most of the staff just sensed his presence, or blamed him for things that happened that they couldn't explain, but one of the cooks claimed to have actually seen him. She said the boy was especially interested when they were making sweet things like pies and cookies.

Did he just want to watch the activity that was probably familiar to him from his time as a living child, or is there something more to this curiosity? Rona thinks possibly the latter. She believes that the boy might actually be able to somehow enjoy the baking.

According to Rona, the historic second Rutherford House on the University of Alberta campus is haunted not only by a famous historical figure, but also a brownie-loving little boy.

"You make some brownie squares and something is there, and either they get it from you eating it, and they get the enjoyment or the flavour from you, or they somehow absorb it from the physical brownie," she said. "I don't know how they do it, but it is very much an attraction for them, just as booze and drugs are for some other spirits."

In addition to the little boy all around the house, Rona also sensed a very strong male presence in the library. The room is gorgeous, with a fireplace, a leather chair, and, of course, books. The little boy wasn't in there, but perhaps it's because the older male presence was both possessive and proud of the library.

"I sort of felt him talking about, you know, 'this is my library.' Just conveying it to me, and then he was gone. But that was fine. I knew it was Mr. Rutherford."

While working on this book, I was talking to Geri Dittrich about the ghost that frequents Walterdale Theatre and she related another interesting story about Rutherford House. She had attended a play with a friend there. As they were waiting for the performance to begin, she and her friend were chatting and having a good time. Once they took their seats, however, Geri looked over at her friend, thinking to find her as she'd been a moment before — cheerful and carefree — but that was not the case. The hair on her friend's arms was standing straight up, her complexion was grey, and if she was breathing, it was so shallow as to be barely noticeable. It was as though she was holding her breath.

Worried, Geri asked her what was wrong.

"He's down there," her friend said in a tiny voice while looking, transfixed, down a hallway. "In front of the door."

But then, as soon as the actors entered the space where she'd been staring, her friend began to breathe again. Her posture relaxed. The goosebumps on her arms disappeared.

"I didn't see him," Geri said. "But she did feel him."

Connecting the Dots

Without knowing what the spirit Geri's friend saw at the end of the hallway looked like, it's impossible to tell whether it could have an actual historical connection to the house. Both the spirits Rona identified in Rutherford House were male, so it's possible that Geri's friend saw one of them, but it's equally possible it was a totally different ghost altogether. We'll never know the answer to that one.

Just as we'll never really know if the spirit of the little boy was actually historically associated with the house. Mr. Rutherford's son, Cecil, was born in 1890, which would mean he was far from being a child when his family moved into the mansion on Saskatchewan Drive. The boy could be a grandchild, but it seems equally likely that he's just a little boy attracted by hustle, bustle, and brownies.

As for Rona seeing someone she took to be Mr. Rutherford himself in his library ... Well, if I had a library as beautiful as his, I'd want to visit it from time to time after my death, too, if I could.

The Quad

History

The Quad doesn't really have a history of its own, the way some of the buildings on campus do, because it's not constructed in the same way. It exists sort of in the negative space between the buildings. If I were feeling fanciful, I might compare it to the negative space between worlds where spirits exist. You know, if I were feeling fanciful.

Encounters

Some time ago, Ben and Rona were called and asked to investigate a private residence in the Clareview neighbourhood. The family had a new baby, and along with every baby comes baby paraphernalia — like baby monitors. Sometimes, the new parents would hear voices coming through their baby monitor, but when they'd rush into the baby's room, there was no one there except the baby, who was far too young to be talking so clearly. Besides, the voices weren't baby voices; usually the parents could hear the voice of an older female voice, and sometimes she was accompanied by a younger male voice.

Rona picked up on the fact that the voices belonged to the spirits of a mother and son. The mother was completely enamoured with the new baby and loved to fuss over it, but the son was very jealous of the attention she was giving the baby and would often try to distract her and make her pay attention to only him. Neither spirit posed a danger to the family, and the new parents were happy to cohabit with the ghosts once they understood all that.

That is an interesting story, but you might well be wondering how it relates to the university. Well, while Rona was at the Clareview residence, investigating the spirits there, the new mother who had called her in told her a story about another ghostly encounter she had had on the university campus.

On the University of Alberta campus, there is a large area of green space surrounded on all sides by various buildings — the Centennial

Centre for Interdisciplinary Science to the north, Assiniboia Hall, Athabasca Hall, and Pembina Hall to the west, the Gunning/Lemieux Chemistry Centre, Central Academic Building, and South Academic Building to the east, and the administration building to the south. That lovely little sheltered green space is called the North Campus Main Quad. It's a fantastic place and looks like something out of Narnia in the wintertime.

It was on one such winter evening, around four or five (which in Edmonton means it was getting dark but wasn't completely dark yet), when the woman was crossing the Quad and saw a man. He was wearing a suit jacket and button-down shirt and was carrying a brief-case and some books. In other words, he wouldn't have looked at all out of place, except that it was wintertime and he wasn't wearing an outdoor jacket. It was possible, since he was hurrying across the Quad just as she was, that he had only a short distance to go and hadn't bothered putting a jacket on.

So, the woman didn't really think too much about him; that is, until he stopped and looked at her in shock. "You can see me," he said.

"Uh, yes," replied the woman, suddenly very confused and wondering if she ought to make for the nearest building entrance, even if it wasn't the right one to get to her class.

"Oh no!" he exclaimed. And then he ran a few more strides away, before disappearing.

Rona, who discussed this encounter with the woman, told me that "[the woman] had the poop scared out of her, and I don't think she made it to her class."

My big question was whether the man had left any footprints. Alas, Rona didn't know the answer, but I prefer to imagine that he did not.

Connecting the Dots

Because there is no real history of the Quad to try to tie the ghost to, it is difficult to find any dots to connect. Rona believes the spirit was most likely that of a professor who used to work on campus. He may or may not have actually died on campus, but either way, she suspects he was hurrying to a class just the same as the woman who spotted him. The fact he was aware that the woman shouldn't have been able to see him suggests to me that he knew he was dead. If that's the case, he was probably not running off to teach the class. Rona agreed with that assessment and said it could be that he wanted to observe a class.

I kind of hope she's right, because that means a love of learning can overcome even death itself. For someone like me, whose husband works in education, that's a nice thought.

Pembina Hall

History

Pembina Hall was built in 1914. It served as a residence for female nursing students and also housed several different classrooms and offices, including anatomy. It is from this department, then housed on the third floor, that the building got the nickname of "the Morgue." Sadly, that nickname became even more appropriate a few years later, in 1918.

The Spanish flu pandemic started right around the same time the First World War ended. Between 1918 and 1919, somewhere between twenty and forty million people fell victim to it — more than died in the Great War — and Canada suffered its fair share of casualties. During the peak of the Spanish flu's devastating run, more people were getting sick than could be treated by the existing medical infrastructure — the hospitals couldn't hold them all. So, oftentimes, other buildings, such as dormitories at the university, served as makeshift hospitals. Pembina Hall was one such building. In late 1918, Pembina Hall was used to treat victims of the Spanish flu. Sometime in 1919 it was converted back to a residence for women, but during its time as a hospital, at least seventy-two people died there.

Despite being nicknamed "the Morgue," Pembina Hall did not have the facilities to deal with the disposal of bodies, and if the hospitals were overrun, one must assume the morgues were as well. Thus, the bodies of flu victims were stored in the basement until they could be collected and dealt with properly. This wasn't a problem during the winter, when it was easy to keep things cool, but in the summer, the basement was reportedly hot and sweltering, which made the bodies decompose quickly. The smell of those decomposing bodies spread throughout the building.

Encounters

The two ghost stories about Pembina Hall are related to the time when the building served as a makeshift hospital. The most famous paranormal occurrence is a horrible odour, much like the smell of a decomposing corpse, that is said to be smelled through its halls on hot summer days.

People also tell the story of a nurse working at Pembina Hall whose soldier boyfriend died of the flu under her care. People have reportedly seen a ghostly couple — she a nurse and he a soldier — wandering the halls of Pembina together. The webpage about the history of Pembina Hall, written by Stacey Bissell, adds an interesting twist to the story.* According to Stacey, the nurse haunts the grounds by herself, searching for her boyfriend. What's more, only men have ever reported seeing her, not women.

Connecting the Dots

Pembina Hall was used as a hospital during the worst of the Spanish flu outbreak in Edmonton, that is without question, and is no doubt the origin of the stories about the smell of death and the sightings of the young nurse (with or without her soldier boyfriend). But whether the historical events have resulted in paranormal activity or have merely primed people's imaginations is tough to say. I wasn't able to track down anyone who had actually witnessed the ghostly nurse to ask them about their experience directly.

------

*   sites.ualberta.ca/~phsa/history.html

- 6 -

Super Dougie's Ink — 6503 118 Avenue NW

History

Doug Lang took over this building for his tattoo studio in August of 2010. It had been empty for a few years before he leased it, but between 1978 and when the building fell empty, it had been occupied by a number of small businesses, including a sign-making company, a computer repair shop, and a hair salon. Originally, however, it had been "B&E Bicycle Repair Shop," and the way Doug came to know that is actually a rather interesting story.

A couple of years ago, Doug happened to go to a neighbourhood garage sale. There, at the back of the garage, leaning up against a wall, was an old business sign for a bicycle repair shop, and it had his business's address on it. Intrigued, Doug struck up a conversation with the woman running the garage sale and found out that the business had originally belonged to her late father. He'd built the building and opened his shop in 1956. He had always been proud of the shop and had spent a lot of time there.

Many of the artifacts discovered when the building was renovated in 2017 clearly date from the time when the building first went up. While they were working, the construction workers discovered a Crush soda bottle from 1956 and an old Edmonton licence plate from 1954. Interestingly, they also found a door hidden behind a wall, complete with its original doorknob and everything. Clearly, at some point in the past when the building was being renovated, someone decided that it was easier to put a wall up in front of the door than to take it out and fill in the hole, but I love the idea of taking down a wall and discovering a door to nowhere within it.

What We Knew Going In

Neither Rona nor I have visited Super Dougie's Ink. This section will be based purely on stories told to me by the tattoo shop's owner and sole employee, Doug Lang.

Encounters

Doug Lang responded to a Facebook post I'd made asking for people from Edmonton to share their ghost stories with me. He said he owned a very small (375 square foot) tattoo parlour and that odd things had happened there — things that had turned him from a paranormal skeptic into a believer. He wasn't sure if his was the kind of story I was looking for because there wasn't one single, big event that had happened, but rather a series of small, odd occurrences that he couldn't find a mundane explanation for.

That, in my experience, is what most people's stories about paranormal experiences or haunted locations actually are: a series of strange little events that add up to something interesting. So, yes, I was very interested in his story and excitedly connected with him to learn more.

As I mentioned, Doug is the only person who works at his tattoo shop and he is the only one with keys to it. Every evening when he's done, he turns all the lights out and leaves, locking the door behind him. The building his shop is in is essentially a rectangle, with the front door at one short end and the light switches on the back wall at the other end. That means after he turns the lights out, he has to walk the length of the building to get out the door, so there is no way he could accidentally leave a light on, not even the bathroom light, because he would have to walk right by it on his way out the door. Despite that, somehow, on several occasions, when he has come in to work in the morning, he has found the bathroom light on.

He has also come in to find the chair that he sits in to tattoo out of place. When he closes up for the night, Doug leaves his chair pretty much in the middle of the room, but he has come in some mornings to find it pushed up against a wall. Before I even had a chance to ask if it could have rolled there by itself, Doug disabused me of that idea. "I wondered if it could have rolled there," he said. "So I tested it."

Doug placed the chair where he would normally leave it before locking up, and tested to see if, given a nudge, it would roll over against the wall where he finds it. It would not. It would roll, but not in that direction. The way the floor is slanted, ever so slightly, the chair would have to go uphill in order to end up where he'd find it. It seems unlikely that it could do that without a little help ... perhaps of the supernatural kind.

Another thing that Doug has noticed, when he comes in some mornings, is the distinct smell of cigar smoke. He doesn't smoke cigars.

By far the oddest thing that happens, and it does so frequently, Doug said, is the radio turning on all by itself. That has happened a handful more times than the light being on without explanation or the chair rolling uphill on its own. It's been witnessed by at least three different people, which Doug finds comforting because if he isn't the only person who is aware of it, it means it isn't just in his head.

Doug isn't disturbed by the radio turning on by itself. At least, not anymore. While it was a bit off-putting at first, Doug thinks that now he might have an explanation for why it's happening.

You see, turning the radio on is one of the last steps of Doug's morning routine, one of the things he does just before opening. Over the years, Doug has noticed that the radio comes on of its own accord when he's a bit behind and is scrambling to get ready to open up for the day. Doug thinks that perhaps the entity who hangs out in his shop is just trying to give him a hand, to do this one task for him so he doesn't have to, or in case he's forgotten.

If Doug is correct, I'm a little bit envious — who couldn't use a helpful spirit to handle some of the more mundane tasks for them on a frenetic morning? I know I certainly could.

Connecting the Dots

Doug thinks there is a spirit inhabiting his shop who likes to help out now and then by turning on the radio when he forgets. It's not only a helpful spirit, but seemingly a friendly one. Neither Doug nor any of his friends who visit him at the shop have ever felt uncomfortable or as though there were negative energies lingering nearby. He wonders if perhaps it is the spirit of the man who originally built this building and ran his bicycle repair shop out of it, but it's difficult to say for sure.

- 7 -

Edmonton's Bluebeard

There are many variations of the story of Bluebeard (most notably "The Robber Bridegroom," "Fitcher's Bird," and "The White Dove"), but the basic premise remains the same in all of them: a rich, older man, feared by most who know him, takes a succession of beautiful young brides and kills them all. The fairy tale is widely believed to have been based on the story of Gilles de Rais, a knight and nobleman from Brittany who fought with Joan of Arc but is most well known as a serial murderer. No doubt you have stumbled across some version of the Bluebeard story in your travels, but did you know that Edmonton has its very own Bluebeard?

Not every ghost gets its own special section, but Edmonton's Bluebeard and Felicia Graham (the section after this one) are different from most because they are associated with several different locations across the city and their stories are somewhat interconnected. Rather than try to pick which section to put them in, I've decided to give them each their own to avoid overly complicating things.

The Bluebeard-esque man who has a connection with Edmonton is most commonly known as James Watson, but he also used several other names, including Walter Andrew Watson, Charles Newton Harvey, James R. Hilton-Huirt, and William B. Huirt. To avoid confusion, I will refer to him as James Watson.

Although some sources cite much higher numbers, according to James's confession he married nineteen women and murdered seven of them.* His usual modus operandi was to place a lonely hearts ad:

> A gentleman, neat in appearance, of courteous dis-
> position, well connected. Has property and connec-
> tions with several corporations, a nice bank account
> and considerable government bonds. Would be
> pleased to correspond with a young lady or widow.
> Object matrimony.**

And then he would woo and marry the women who responded, telling them that he had to travel frequently for work, when in reality he mostly had to travel frequently to keep his other wives occupied while he bilked them and their families for as much money as he could get. He would write their families, asking for money for him to invest; he would also have his wives (many of them from well-off families or with money of their own) write up wills naming him sole beneficiary. He would also create a will, naming the women as his sole beneficiary, but those amounted to nothing more than a cover to make the women feel more comfortable in their relationship — he knew he was going to outlive them.

Watson didn't murder all of his wives, although he was tempted to kill even some who survived his attention. Speaking of one of his first wives, Katherine Kruse, Watson said in his confession, "No violence attempted on her — had impulse but was able to resist."***

Those women he was unable to resist the urge to kill died in a variety of horrible ways, most involving bludgeoning and/or water.

Marie Austin was beaten with a rock and dumped into Lake Coeur d'Alene. An unnamed Seattle lady he murdered by pushing over a

---

* murderpedia.org/male.W/w/watson-james.htm

** kimberleybulletin.com/opinion/the-horrifying-marriage-
career-of-james-bluebeard-watson

*** murderpedia.org/male.W/w/watson-james.htm

waterfall. He drowned Beatrice Andrewartha in Lake Washington; Elizabeth Prior, he bludgeoned to death with a hammer. The same fate awaited Bertha Goodrich, whom Watson bludgeoned to death and then threw into Lake Washington. His next victim, Alice Ludvigson, "fell" out of a boat and drowned in the St. Joe River near Spokane, Washington, and Nina Delany was strangled, bludgeoned, and slashed with a knife in Los Angeles County.

Some accounts add another two or three women to the list of his victims, claiming that he also admitted to killing Agnes Wilson, whom he drowned in Lake Washington; Eleanor Frazier, whom he threw into a river, letting its current carry her over a waterfall where she was crushed on the rocks below; and M.A. Watt, whom he drowned in Lake Coeur d'Alene.

Over time, the frequency of Watson's crimes began to escalate, meaning that more and more women were in danger. So, one can only be thankful that one of his wives, Kathryn Wombacher, became suspicious of her husband. Thinking that he might be cheating on her, she hired a private detective to follow him, and that was when things began to unravel for the serial killer.

For me, one of the most interesting aspects of this Bluebeard story is that in the fairy tales, there is almost always a locked door that Bluebeard's wives are forbidden to open. In this true-life story, Watson had a locked black bag that his wives were forbidden to open.

In the fairy tale, once the locked door was open, all of Bluebeard's crimes were revealed in some way or another. In real life, once authorities opened Watson's locked bag, it revealed all the souvenirs he had kept from his victims, thus shining a light on his many crimes.

All the murders James Watson confessed to and was convicted of took place between 1918 and 1920, occurring in several different locations in the United States. Two of his wives, however, were from Edmonton. What's more, according to a May 10, 2014, *Edmonton Journal* article by Chris Zdeb, between 1915 and 1919, Watson actually lived part time in Edmonton, at the Arlington Apartments.

The Arlington was home to the serial killer James P. Watson, sometimes called "Edmonton's Bluebeard."

There are many people who believe Watson killed far more women than he admitted to, but in May 1920, he was taken off the streets and confined to San Quentin, where he was reportedly a model prisoner until he died of pneumonia on October 15, 1939. He was sixty-one.

– 8 –

Felicia Graham

Anyone with even a passing interest in the ghost stories of Edmonton is likely familiar with the name Felicia Graham. Felicia's story takes place in the early 1900s. She was a beautiful young woman from a well-to-do family; she moved to Edmonton from out east after finishing a master's degree at the University of Toronto. Felicia lived and worked for a time as a teacher in British Columbia, but then eventually moved to Edmonton and accepted a teaching position at Westmount Junior High School in 1918.*

Felicia was not happy at Westmount. Not only was she making less money in her position there than at her previous job in New Westminster, B.C., but she was also making less than her male colleagues. It wasn't fair and she wasn't going to stand for it. Felicia stood up for herself and her right to equal pay, and eventually the school board agreed to give her a new position, across the river at Strathcona High School.**

Unfortunately, before Felicia could begin her new job, the Spanish flu pandemic reached Edmonton. As a result, all the schools were

---

* seeksghosts.blogspot.com/2015/06/edmontons-felicia-graham.html

** citymuseumedmonton.ca/2014/07/21/the-strange-disappearance-of-felicia-graham

Felicia Graham, who disappeared in 1918, is the subject of many local urban legends and ghost stories. What really happened to her?

closed and many of them converted to temporary hospitals. Felicia herself became ill with the flu early on but quickly recovered. Some reports say she then went on to volunteer as a nurse in the care centres, although it's tough to know for sure how accurate that is. What we do know with certainty is that when the schools reopened in 1919, Felicia did not report to work.

An investigation revealed that the last time Felicia was seen alive was when she left her luxury apartment in the LeMarchand Mansion (11523 100 Avenue NW) on November 15, 1918. She was wearing, according to a March 31, 1919, article in the *Edmonton Bulletin*, a "dark green dress and dark green coat and dark green sailor hat; mink furs; and No. 7 black lace boots."

A witness said they saw Felicia, dressed that way, standing in the middle of the High Level Bridge. It's not unusual that she would have been on that bridge, as she would have needed to cross it to get from her apartment to where she worked at Strathcona High School. What was unusual, however, was that the witness said they saw her standing in the middle of the bridge, and then she just vanished.

Had she jumped? Fallen? Been pushed? Her family didn't believe so. In fact, they offered a $500 reward — a significant amount of money in 1919 — for information about her disappearance. According to the *Edmonton Bulletin* article, her family "feared she may have suffered a relapse of influenza and wandered away," perhaps to die in the bush that surrounded the city. They put forward another idea, too: as she spoke several languages very well, they wondered if she might have befriended and taken refuge in the home of a foreign family.

By April 12, 1919, there hadn't been any new leads and the *Edmonton Bulletin* published an article with the title "Assistance to Miss Graham's Family Urged." The article mostly reiterated the fact Felicia was missing, and that her family, fearing she had wandered away while ill, was offering a reward for news about her. A week later, the city took things up a notch and offered its own $200 reward. This was a reward of a slightly different sort, however, because it was specifically for the recovery of Felicia's body. The article included a note that her family's reward, which had previously been for her recovery alive or for news about her, now also included a $200 reward for anyone who found her body.

About two weeks after that, around midnight on April 27, the police were called out to the river after some boys reported that they had seen the body of a woman they thought could be Felicia Graham, floating near the bridge. Unfortunately, by the time the police arrived, it was very dark and the current had pulled the body away and they were unable to locate it.

If that was Felicia's body the boys spotted, and I believe it was, it seems that it continued on down the river. On May 6, 1919, the *Edmonton Bulletin* had a tiny little article on its front page. The headline read "Body of Miss Graham Has Been Recovered." The entirety of the text was, "The body of the late Miss Graham has been found by her brother, north of Vermilion, and will be taken east to her old home in Lindsay, Ont., for burial."

A later article in the paper, published on May 8, clarified things, stating that a man named William Markowsky had found Felicia's body. I suspect that perhaps her brother had identified her and the newspaper chose an unclear verb in the original death notification.

According to the May 8 article, Felicia's body was found near Hopkins Ferry, just north of Vermilion, on the afternoon of Monday, May 5. The article goes on to state that the body was carefully examined and a coroner's inquest was held. Evidence was given regarding the state of her corpse and the circumstances around her disappearance — including, it is noted specifically in the article, the fact Felicia had plans for the future. Given all that information, the jury decided that her cause of death was accidental drowning.

I believe the article, and presumably the jury, made special note of the fact that Ms. Graham had plans for the future to make the case that it was unlikely she had jumped off the bridge rather than fallen. In 1919, suicide would have been a scandalous way to die, and I suspect most families (then and now, perhaps) would prefer that a loved one's cause of death be accidental rather than intentional.

Felicia's story is potentially complicated by the fact that James (Bluebeard) Watson lived in Edmonton at the same time she did. He lived here, on and off, between 1915 and 1919, and Felicia disappeared on November 15, 1918. It is possible that she ran afoul of Mr. Watson and became one of his victims.

I don't believe that is the case, however.

First, Watson confessed to murdering many of his wives, but he did not include Felicia in the list, even though he was going to prison for the rest of his life and would have had nothing to lose by naming her. Second, it doesn't fit his MO. He was not someone to just happen across a random woman and throw her off a bridge. Watson married his victims, milked them and their families for money, and then killed him. No one has ever claimed that Felicia was married, nor had she or Watson approached her family to ask for money, to "invest" — as he claimed was his intent with his previous wives — or even for reward money for information about her disappearance.

No. Although claiming that Felicia ran afoul of Edmonton's Bluebeard makes for a good story, I think it is more likely that she either fell or jumped from the bridge on that November day.

In November, the river would have been very cold. It might not have been frozen enough to walk on, but it probably would have sported some ice. If a person were to fall from the High Level Bridge and die, it is likely that their body would have broken through the ice. It would have decomposed slowly because of the temperature, and it might have remained trapped beneath ice for the whole of the winter. By the end of April, however, the water would have warmed, the ice melted, and the build-up of gases in the body would probably have been enough to bring it to the surface and send it down the river. I think this is the most likely explanation for the delayed discovery of Felicia's body after her disappearance. Her body was likely trapped beneath the ice until the thaw; once that happened, the corpse floated to the surface, was spotted in April, and then eventually pulled from the river in May.

The question is: how did she get in the river? I don't believe she was pushed, because the witness who saw her on the bridge did not at any time mention another person with her. They simply said she was there, and then she was gone. I think that description of events is most consistent with her falling or jumping.

Which one of those was it? I wouldn't even want to begin to guess.

The idea that Felicia would not possibly kill herself because she had plans for the future, was well educated, and seemed like a happy person might have seemed plausible in 1919, but in 2019 we know that depression can strike anyone at any time and that you can never tell from the outside looking in how someone else is really feeling.

That being said, there is also no reason to believe it any more likely that Felicia jumped than that she slipped on an iced-over bridge deck and, still weak from the Spanish flu, which was an especially brutal strain, fell over the side.

We'll never know the truth about that, but at least Felicia's family learned that she had died and her body was returned to them. People say that closure is overrated, but I'd think it certainly beats never knowing if your child is alive or dead.

– 9 –

Westmount Junior High School — 11124 130 Street NW

History

When forward-thinking city planners commissioned Westmount School back in 1912, the area surrounding it was almost completely undeveloped bush.* Wet, undeveloped bush, actually. According to the Edmonton City as Museum Project website, when the school first opened in 1915, under Principal John Scoffield, it was all alone in the middle of a marshy field. The area was so marshy, in fact, that reaching the school could be difficult, and in wet weather, makeshift bridges were used to navigate the mud and water.

As an aside, I can tell you that to this day you do not want to try and shortcut across the school field in the spring if you can avoid it. For those who can't avoid it, it's best to make use of the sheet of plywood that is often laid across the giant mudhole at the southwest corner of the gymnasium.

In 1918, Westmount School was chosen to be the first junior high school in Edmonton. That same year, the Spanish flu was devastating

---

* citymuseumedmonton.ca/2015/08/25/westmount-school

the city. All the public schools were closed and several, including Westmount, were converted into temporary hospitals. It was during this period that the inciting incident in Felicia Graham's story takes place, but as you'll recall, Felicia was looking for a transfer away from Westmount Junior High School, not to it.

Over the years, a great many renovations and expansions have been made to the school to meet the changing needs and population of the neighbourhood it serves. It has never, however, been a boarding school.

What We Knew Going In

I walk by Westmount Junior High every time I go to get my groceries. Well, almost every time. Sometimes I take a different route, but the front doors of the school have little grotesques (stone statues of faces) at the front door, and one of them is a Pokémon GO PokéStop so I usually choose a route that takes me by the school. Not only because it helps me play one of my favourite video games, but also because it's a beautiful building. I've never been inside it, but its Gothic, red-brick exterior and tall centre tower are very striking against a blue sky.

Rona, on the other hand, has spent a great deal of time inside this school. Not only as part of an official paranormal investigation, but also as a student. For a short while, some of MacEwan University's (then called Grant MacEwan College) art courses were taught out of this building, and Rona attended them as a student. So, we do have an extensive amount of exposure to it.

Encounters

The most well-known spirit said to haunt Westmount Junior High is that of teacher Felicia Graham. People claim to have seen her incorporeal form wandering the hallways, or to have heard the click of her heels as she entered her old classroom.

There's also another, less known story, about a boy named Harold, who is said to have been accidentally locked in the central tower and either jumped or fell to his death trying to escape. The stories never really seem to specify *how* Harold haunts the school, just that he does.

Rona investigated this location in a rather large group — a couple of men who were in the Canadian Armed Forces, their partners and some of their friends, plus Ben and Rona. They gained access to the school because a teacher one of their guests knew got them in.

"It wasn't one hundred percent sanctioned," Rona told me.

This is a phrase, and idea, I've become quite familiar with when it comes to paranormal investigations. Often, investigators (in general, not just Rona) have consent from *someone* to be in a building (a night guard or a teacher, for example) but they don't necessarily have consent from *everyone* responsible for that building (the owner, the school board, etc.).

The group went at night, excited because one of the men from the Canadian Armed Forces — let's call him Kai — was an expert in sound. Specifically, Rona said, "In recording, analyzing, and evaluating, you know, whether it's human or not human."

The little group split up into several smaller groups.

I want to stop and make a joke right here about how anyone who has ever watched a scary movie (or even *Scooby-Doo*) knows that splitting up is never a very good idea — except I can't. When Rona recounts stories of investigations and paranormal encounters, she frequently says things like, "There were too many people there for me to get a good fix on the spirit." What I've taken away from those conversations is that if you are scared and don't want to encounter anything, staying in a large group is the way to go. If, however, your ultimate goal is to have a meaningful encounter with the ghost, the fewer people or distractions around you, the better.

So, they split up. Kai and his friend, whom we'll call Lucas, headed all the way up to the tower so they could investigate the story about Harold.

The story that Rona heard, which she does not believe to be true, is based on the claim that at some point the school was a boarding school, and that the kids lived there full time and attended school, but they got to go home on the holidays. Unfortunately, one kid (Harold, we presume) either didn't have a family to go home to, or he didn't want to go home to them. Whatever the case may have been, he hid when it was time to leave. As the story goes, he found himself alone in the school and somehow trapped in the tower over the Christmas holidays. In this version of the story, Harold died of thirst or starvation.

Although Rona doesn't believe that the story of Harold is true, Kai and Lucas wanted to check it out, so they went as far up the tower as they could. While they were up there, they got several good orb photos, and both reported feeling uneasy, but they didn't see or hear anything more substantial than that.

Even Rona, who is especially sensitive to these sorts of things, couldn't quite "get a handle" on any spirits in the areas she investigated. She could feel there was a spirit in the school, but she couldn't get any specific details at all.

That wasn't Rona's only visit to the school, of course. As mentioned, years before, MacEwan University taught some of its art classes there on a sort of satellite campus. Rona attended those classes and remembers the strong feeling of being watched by something she couldn't see but that raised the hairs on her arms and the back of her neck. And she wasn't alone. A couple of her other classmates felt the same, but they only ever spoke about it in whispers.

Connecting the Dots

Rona is confident that there is a spirit at Westmount School, but she's also confident that it is not the spirit of Felicia Graham. I, of course, have no way to judge that, but I tend to think that if Felicia Graham were going to choose a place to haunt, it probably wouldn't be the school she didn't even want to work at.

Aside from the tangential connection to the Felicia Graham story, Westmount School has a pretty unremarkable history, so I don't see any particular reason to assume that whoever, or whatever, haunts it is actually going to show up in any history textbooks. Perhaps someday Rona will get another chance to visit it in a smaller group and learn more, but until then, I think it will have to remain a mystery.

10

Charles Camsell Hospital — 12804 114 Avenue NW

History

Construction on the existing building that houses the most recent incarnation of the Charles Camsell Hospital began in 1964, and the hospital opened its doors in July 1967. That wasn't the first building — nor the first hospital — to occupy those grounds, however.

The original building that eventually became the Charles Camsell Hospital was built by Jesuits in 1913 and operated as a Jesuit college until 1942. Then, when the Second World War began, the U.S. Army bought the property and used it as a sort of staging ground while they built the Alaska Highway. During this time, they erected several new buildings.

By 1944, their business was done, so the Americans sold the property to the Canadian government. The government constructed a series of tunnels and corridors to connect the new outbuildings the Americans had built to the main building.

Originally, the federal government had intended to use the hospital to treat Canadian soldiers returning from war overseas but,

After it stopped functioning as a hospital, the Charles Camsell Hospital sat empty for quite some time. Interestingly, some parts of it had power during this period, and some parts did not.

despite some protests, it was instead turned into a tuberculosis (TB) hospital to serve Inuit and other Indigenous Peoples from Alberta and the northern territories. It officially opened in this capacity on August 26, 1946, and was named after the famous geologist Dr. Charles Camsell.

By 1964 the original Jesuit college building was getting a bit old (by Alberta standards) and was beginning to need more maintenance. Instead of providing that, the government began construction on a new building on the same property. This building became the home of the hospital. The old Jesuit college building was torn down. The new hospital building was called a "Centennial gift to the North" in an *Edmonton Journal* article from October 11, 1967. That building is the one that continues to stand on the property to this day.

The Charles Camsell Hospital operated as a hospital for Indigenous patients from 1946 until the 1970s. Reading through newspaper reports from the time, I found a lot of praise heaped on the hospital and its staff (from Indigenous people and others), but I also found reports of concerns about racism, poor practices, and surgery without consent and under inadequate anesthesia. However good the intentions of most individuals associated with the hospital, there is no question that horrible things occurred there during this dark time in Canadian history.

Between 1928 and 1972, nearly three thousand women in Alberta were involuntarily sterilized under the Sexual Sterilization Act. Many of these forced sterilizations occurred at the Charles Camsell Hospital.*

Sterilization was not the hospital's primary function, however. During the years it served as a hospital for Indigenous people, the Camsell's main purpose was to treat TB in that population. During this time, treatments for TB typically consisted of either rest therapy or highly invasive surgeries that sound worse than the disease itself — treatments like removing ribs, or collapsing part of the patient's lung. To make matters worse, some of these procedures occurred while the patients were under only local, not general, anesthetic. In other words, they were awake the whole time.

Streptomycin was discovered in 1943 and was being used, along with other drugs taken orally, like isoniazid and para-aminosalicylic acid, to treat TB by the 1950s. For some time, however, it continued to be used alongside surgical treatments.

By 1959, a time when the medicine existed to treat patients with TB through medications taken orally, at least one man (then a child of sixteen), Dave Melting Tallow, was not treated orally but instead underwent lung resection under local anesthetic. "They removed three ribs," he told Dr. Maureen Lux in 2016. "And they removed part of my lung.... They used a saw. I was awake and I could hear the saw. They got partway and then they told me, 'now we're breaking the ribs off' ... When they did that, it felt like someone hit you inside the

---

* ammsa.com/publications/windspeaker/sterilization-victims-urged-come-forward-0

chest. And they did that three times. I just heard the saw buzzing away and cutting stuff."*

The hospital didn't just treat patients who came to it voluntarily. Teams assembled by the government regularly flew out to remote Indigenous communities. There, they would test people for TB, and if they showed any signs of the disease, they would be flown back to the hospital to be treated. Sometimes forcibly.

Those patients, young and old, were taken from their families and kept in a hospital far from home. Many stayed at the Camsell for years. Many never left. Patients from remote communities who died at the hospital often didn't even have their remains returned home. That left many families with unanswered questions and a significant lack of closure.

In 1990, a cairn listing the names of ninety-eight First Nations people who died at the Camsell between 1946 and 1966 was unveiled at St. Albert Aboriginal Cemetery. Even those names can provide only partial closure, though, because many people have no idea where their deceased family members are buried.

By the 1970s, TB treatments had advanced to the point where the disease was controlled well enough that there was no longer a need for a dedicated hospital in Alberta. Thus, the Camsell's purview shifted from being a TB hospital to serving as a general treatment hospital.

Many deaths occurred at the hospital, as they do at any hospital; however, one death in particular stands out. In June of 1982, twenty-two-year-old Kevin Crandall was resurfacing a section of the hospital's roof when he fell to his death. According to the *Edmonton Journal*, no one witnessed the accident, but investigators determined that he was on the roof, winching a bucket of gravel down, when a hoist broke free and fell, taking him with it. The story of this man's tragic death helped to fuel the rumour mill regarding ghosts and suspicious happenings in and around the hospital. People expect deaths to occur at a hospital, but not in that particular manner.

* canadashistory.ca/explore/canada-s-history-forum/researching-and-revealing-indian-hospitals-in-canada/transcript

The hospital continued to function for a decade more, slowly winding down its operations (the pediatrics unit closed in 1993, and the emergency room closed in 1994). It closed for good in 1996.

The hospital was then rented out to production companies and used to film several projects, including Dave Thomas's movie *Whitecoats*, and the horror movie *Ginger Snaps 2*. Even long after its closure, some parts of the hospital looked completely functional; other parts, however, were showing the results of being ignored for several years. The disparity between these parts of the hospital has led to some of the sense of discontinuity that urban and paranormal explorers talk about when discussing the Camsell.

In 2004, developer Gene Dub purchased the property with the intention of turning it into residential units — just more than one hundred apartments were envisioned for the hospital building itself, and several low-rise or townhouse units were to be built on the surrounding grounds. The project has been plagued with problems, though — legal and financial, the discovery of asbestos that needed removing, and not one but two fires.

The first fire took place in 2006. One morning, when I dropped my daughter off at school (about a block away from the hospital), I discovered the Camsell was on fire. I asked her teacher if there were any concerns about that, especially given the exceptionally high amount of asbestos in the hospital, and she assured me there were not. So I went home. I hadn't been home long when the school called to advise me that they were evacuating the children to a different location because of concerns about air quality and that if I hurried, I could pick up my daughter right then and save myself the hassle of finding her at a different location later.

I ran to the school just in time to see her bus driving away. It paused for long enough for her teacher to yell out the door to tell me where I could eventually find my daughter.

I was so frustrated.

My frustrations were incredibly minor compared with those of the firefighters who were trying to control the fire at the hospital. You see, they'd entered the building only to find it was not safe for them to be there. Someone had set up booby traps and obstacles to try and dissuade vagrants and explorers. When *Edmonton Sun* reporter Eliza Barlow spoke to fire department spokesman Nikki Booth, Nikki said the fire crews "encountered barbed wire on the stairwells and on the walls, holes in the floors, boarded-up rooms."* As a result, they couldn't fight the fire from the inside and had to use aerial ladders and hoses to fight it externally.

The fire started when a stray spark caused by a renovation crew cutting through a metal beam ignited some nearby insulation. A second fire, this time in 2014, was started the same way: a stray spark lighting insulation. That fire was far less dramatic than the first, with no reports of booby traps or barbed-wire staircases.

In July 2018, multiple newspapers reported that developer Gene Dub expected to have units completed by the spring of 2019. However, as of July 2019, the site remains under construction. This pattern of postponed milestones and slow progress is one that neighbourhood residents are used to, even if they don't particularly like it.

If the units had been ready by spring of 2019 as projected, it would have been fifteen years from the time that Dub first purchased the property until he finally completed the first major step of his vision for developing the former Charles Camsell Hospital. As it is, it looks like both he and the surrounding neighbourhood will have to wait until at least 2020 for that to happen.

What We Knew Going In

I actually met Rona while I was researching this hospital for *Haunted Hospitals: Eerie Tales About Hospitals, Sanatoriums, and Other Institutions*. So, by the time I began writing this book, I was very familiar with this hospital, as was Rona. Looking back at what I had known before I began writing *that* book … I had heard rumours. A lot of rumours. The Charles Camsell Hospital is in my neighbourhood,

---

* *Edmonton Sun*, November 18, 2006.

and around here, people usually refer to it as either "the Camsell" or "the Haunted Hospital," and it's understood that the terms can be used interchangeably. Before I started doing research, I'd heard stories about experimental treatments being performed in the hospital and of mass graves somewhere on the property.

Long before meeting me and helping me with *Haunted Hospitals*, Rona had investigated the Camsell on two separate occasions and also researched its history.

Encounters

Rumours and vague stories about how haunted the Charles Camsell Hospital is are rampant. Anyone who lives anywhere near Edmonton, is interested in local history and urban exploration (exploring abandoned buildings), or has any connection to the Camsell has heard them. A quick Google search will turn up dozens. One of my favourites came as a comment on a post about the hospital on the *It's Not Always About Me* blog.* There, someone with the username Thelma Kim relates a story about when she was a little girl and hospitalized at the Charles Camsell. She was in bed when a "lovely Native woman" bathed in light appeared. The woman looked a lot like Thelma Kim's mother, so Thelma wasn't afraid and chatted happily with her. Then, when her mother actually came into the room, the other woman vanished as suddenly as she'd appeared. Years later, Thelma went up north to be with her mother and learn some family history. One evening, they were looking through family pictures and Thelma saw her maternal grandmother for the first time. She looked exactly like the woman who had visited her at the hospital when she was five. She later learned that her grandmother had died at the Charles Camsell in 1970 — a decade before Thelma saw her there.

When Mark Leslie and I were writing *Haunted Hospitals*, Jocelyn Chisaakay told me a story that also involved learning intriguing details while speaking about her family history. Jocelyn and her friend Tara

---

* itsnotalwaysaboutme-lauren.blogspot.com/2010/10/abandoned-cameron-camsell-hospital.html

were walking by the hospital late one night. Snow was on the ground and Jocelyn remembers being cold and unhappy.

Seeing the hospital, Tara wanted to go inside to take a look, but even just the idea made Jocelyn's heart pound in her chest. She didn't know why; this wasn't a fear that made sense or that she'd ever experienced before, but she didn't even want to look at the hospital. Tara was persistent, however, and kept trying to get Jocelyn to go in. Tara tugged her across the street, but as soon as they reached the trees that edge the property, a long, scary howl cut through the night. It was coming from the hospital.

"Did you hear that?" Jocelyn remembered asking Tara.

"I heard it," Tara said.

Any thoughts about exploring the hospital were abandoned, and the two girls hurried away. Still, Jocelyn couldn't forget the howl. It sounded like someone in pain. She wanted to know who or what had made it. Further, why had she been afraid to even look at the hospital? That wasn't like her.

Years later, when she moved back to her reservation, she told the story of her and Tara's Camsell encounter to her father. He told her that her grandfather had passed away in that hospital. "Perhaps," her father said, "he just wanted to say hello."

Jocelyn conceded that was possible, but if it was her grandfather just saying hello, why was it so frightening?

People who, unlike Jocelyn, have entered the hospital have reported all sorts of things, from a room covered in blood to strange noises, and feeling like they were being watched.

Ben and Rona had heard stories about the Charles Camsell Hospital as well. They became intrigued and decided to investigate. In the end, they made two separate investigatory visits to the hospital, one during the day and one at night. They weren't officially allowed to be on the property for either visit, but they'd made friends with one of the security guards and he let them in.

At the time of their first visit, there was an outbuilding on the west end of the property that connected to the main building through an underground tunnel. They used that tunnel to enter the main building for their daytime investigation. The outbuilding has since been razed (and the tunnel filled in, presumably), but I've read a lot of accounts of urban and paranormal explorers entering the hospital, and that tunnel has a starring role in many of them. It seems it was an easier way in than through the heavily locked and chained front doors.

Emerging from the dark tunnel into the hospital was a surreal experience. There was, of course, a change in light levels, but more importantly there was the fact that the hospital had been used as a set for several movies. So although some parts of it were derelict and neglected, some appeared to be fully functioning. As if they were just waiting for a patient to come rolling through the doors.

There was an old operating room that fell somewhere in between those two categories. It had electricity and some equipment in it, but it wasn't fully set up like a movie set. One intriguing thing about the room was a light panel, like the kind a doctor would use to view an X-ray. When Ben and Rona looked at it through their infrared camera, they could see it was glowing. This despite the fact that it was actually turned off. Ben wasn't sure whether the glowing was paranormal in origin, the result of something mundane, like an electrical short, or just a light bulb acting up, but it was interesting nonetheless. Especially as the light wasn't flickering or flashing — it was pulsing.

Rona and Ben turned on an audio recorder and set it on a metal shelf in the room, not far from the pulsing light panel, and then left the room. In fact, they left the floor. "Like, literally," Rona told me, "there was nobody on that floor. It was just us in the building."

Still, despite the fact that there were no other breathing human beings anywhere in the building, when they eventually returned and played back the tape, they discovered all sorts of unexplained noises.

What's more, the recorder had been moved. It had been knocked over.

When they listened to the recording, Rona and Ben could hear the sound of people moving around, something that sounded like metal tools being shifted around on a tray, and a very loud bang, like someone slamming their hand down on the metal shelf on which Rona and Ben had left the recorder. Had this been why the recorder was knocked over?

The most dramatic evidence they caught on that recording, though, was the sound of an authoritative male voice calling out for "Karen." Ben and Rona thought the voice might belong to a doctor calling out to a nurse but, of course, they couldn't possibly be sure. Still, they'd collected enough evidence that they definitely wanted to return for a second trip. This time at night.

Ben and Rona went in the front doors for the nighttime investigation, but they were not alone. They'd brought a whole group of people along with them, including a film crew. The Charles Camsell Hospital is a big building and they had a limited amount of time to investigate it (as their being there wasn't "100 percent sanctioned"), plus they wanted to document as much of their investigation as they could. The more people and cameras they could have on the premises, the better.

Before they went into the hospital, Rona gathered everyone together outside the front door to perform a protection ceremony. While she was in the midst of the ceremony, the security guard who was letting them in came over to observe. His presence, looming over them, scratching his butt, and even spitting up a huge glob of phlegm, inspired Rona to cut the protection ceremony short. One wonders if things might have gone a whole lot differently if she hadn't …

Once they were inside the hospital, the large group split up into smaller ones. Rona and Ben's group took an elevator downstairs to one of the most obvious destinations for a paranormal investigator — the morgue. There were actually two elevators side by side in the hallway, one with power and one without. Obviously, they took the one that was operational.

Poking around the morgue, they discovered some interesting things — there was still equipment in the room, left behind from when the hospital was in operation or functioning as a movie set — but nothing out of the ordinary or paranormal. Disappointed, they were about to leave and move on to a different area when they heard the "ding" of the elevator and the sound of its doors opening out in the hallway. Peering out, expecting to see more members of their group appear, they were surprised to find it wasn't the elevator they'd come down in that had its doors open, but rather the non-operational one. That one that didn't even have power.

When they drew nearer to get a better look, the doors closed and the elevator — with no power and no passenger — began to go up.

"Where would we have ended up if we'd gotten in?" Ben wondered aloud as he told me the story. I can't help but wish they'd moved a little bit faster so we'd know the answer to that question.

While Rona and Ben's group was in the morgue, another group was upstairs on the fourth floor, dealing with a different unseen presence. As the group explored, they suddenly heard really loud footsteps above them. Initially, they suspected it was just someone walking around on the fifth floor, but then they realized that even if there was someone on the floor above them, they wouldn't be able to hear them. Hospital floors are thick. Sound doesn't carry through them in the same way it might in a private residence.

A couple of the smaller groups met up soon afterward, in another obvious destination for a paranormal explorer: the psych ward. This area had a lot to offer all the investigators, but especially Rona.

As they were exploring this area of the hospital, they found themselves in a section with several office-type areas, set off the main area by Plexiglas windows. As they were leaving, someone in their group said, "Were those handprints there before?"

Looking at the glass, the group could see handprints that streaked down the window. Unfortunately, they couldn't be sure the handprints hadn't been there when they first arrived on the floor, nor could they say for sure that what had put them there wasn't mundane in nature.

Looking down a hallway in the surgical wing of the Charles Camsell Hospital.

Even so, the group found it unsettling to see the handprints, and it put several people on edge.

Soon after that, some members of their party could smell smoke. "We were kinda arguing about if it was pipe or cigar [smoke]," Ben told me. "Cigars smell nasty, whereas pipes are more pleasant.... I smelled cigar but some said it was a pipe."

Probably unrelated to the smell of smoke — although who knows, really — Rona also encountered the first of several visible manifestations of a ghost on that same floor. This was a teenage Caucasian girl with long brown hair, who was wearing a hospital gown. Rona described her as being in "an incredible amount of emotional pain." Possibly, as evidence of that, her wrists were wrapped with bandages, but Rona didn't believe her suicide attempt had been successful.

When I asked Rona if she could pinpoint what era the spirit was from, she said her impression was the late 1970s. Rona couldn't tell if the girl had actually died in the hospital at some point, or died elsewhere and come back to the Camsell because she believed she belonged there. Although I'm still extremely skeptical about the existence of ghosts, the storyteller in me wants to suggest that perhaps the girl had received aid at the hospital in life, and then, when she found herself trapped on Earth in death, she thought the hospital was a logical place to find help once again.

Rona said that when the girl moved, she hung her head, allowing her long hair to obscure her face, hiding herself away from the living world, or maybe shielding herself from it. She was quite twitchy and kept scratching herself, deep enough to leave deep welts.

"When are Mom and Dad coming to pick me up?" the girl asked. She kept repeating that, over and over. If Rona asked her a question, the girl would just ignore her and keep saying, "When are Mom and Dad coming to pick me up?"

Rona says that at first the girl seemed to think the little party of investigators would be able to help her, so she stuck around, but when she realized that only Rona could see her and no one there had the power at that time to help her, she faded away.

So did several members of the group. Not literally faded away, of course, but they split off into three groups to explore other parts of the hospital. One of those groups stayed on the psych ward, the second group included Rona, and the third included Ben and his friend Darin.

The three separate groups hadn't been out of each other's sights for long when the walkie-talkies started to act up. Everyone in all three groups heard an unearthly scream of pain or horror come through the walkie-talkies. (Was it the same scream that Jocelyn had heard that night she and her friend ventured onto the hospital grounds?) The scream was immediately followed by Darin's voice over the line. "Leslie, are you there?" he asked. "Leslie? Are you okay? Leslie, are you there?"

Leslie was Darin's girlfriend, so it would make sense for him to want to be sure she was okay after hearing a horrific scream. The only thing was that Leslie wasn't at the hospital. She wasn't even in the country that night. Oh, and Darin didn't have a walkie-talkie. Oh! And also? Only some people heard his voice come over the walkie-talkies; everyone else heard only static.

As you can imagine, everyone in their group was pretty on edge by that point, but that uneasiness drove them to explore more — there was no talk of turning back or leaving early, and the small subgroups carried on.

One of them went to the former pediatric floor. There, they spread a sheet of plastic on the floor, placed a ball in the centre, and covered the surrounding area with baby powder. The idea was that if a spirit wanted to play with the ball, it might leave some sort of evidence in the powder. Alternatively, if the ball moved by itself, it would also leave marks. The group set up an infrared camera to record the scene and then carried on with their explorations.

When they returned to see whether their little spirit trap had captured any evidence of the paranormal, they found the ball in the exact same place they'd left it and no ghostly child footprints or anything of that nature in the baby powder. No doubt they were disappointed … right up until they watched the footage recorded by their infrared camera.

The visual footage wasn't the star of that story; it was the audio that the camera had captured that really amazed Rona.

"You heard the elevator doors close," Rona said — perhaps the sound of the paranormal explorers on that elevator leaving the floor. "And as soon as those elevator doors closed, it [the floor] came alive. You could hear somebody pushing a medical cart, you could hear the beep, beep, beep of a heart machine … you could hear all this stuff just like the [whole floor] was operating again."

Meanwhile, as all this audio activity was taking place, the camera just continued to record the ball sitting in place in the middle of the plastic. Then, suddenly, something unseen struck the camera and moved it slightly off to the left.

Alas, the video evidence was destroyed when someone used the wrong tape to record a television sitcom. When that was discovered, I

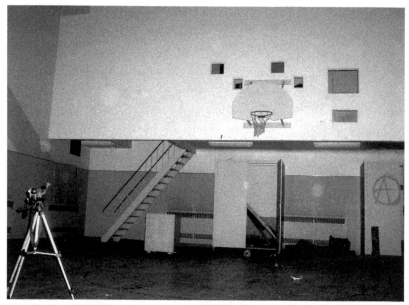

A room in the Charles Camsell Hospital. Rona encountered spirits here during her overnight investigation of the location.

can only imagine that the scene was even more dramatic than the one recorded on the tape!

Rona's group decided to head back down to the basement. That was where they discovered an auditorium. It had two projection booths, basketball hoops, and a variety of different equipment. It was also occupied. Not just by one ghost, but by many.

Rona says when she went down there she encountered a whole bunch of Indigenous peoples' spirits. "And," she said, "they were feeling everything between angry, sad, despairing — every emotion possible except anything positive."

Out of all the ghosts down there, one in particular caught Rona's attention and tugged at her heartstrings. It was the spirit of an Indigenous Elder; he was sitting on a bench against the wall, away from most of the other spirits. He was holding his head in his hands, but when Rona approached him, he looked up and met her gaze. "We did not ask to be here," he said. "We don't want to be here anymore."

The last place Rona checked out before calling it a night was one of the offices on the main floor. She and a woman named Stephanie went to go look through them. Now, one thing Rona repeats pretty frequently when she's talking about paranormal investigations is that even though things might be frightening, if you're not willing to face your fears and keep looking, you shouldn't be there. It doesn't make any sense, she thinks, to seek out paranormal activity and then run away as soon as you find it. It also doesn't make any sense to put yourself in unnecessarily dangerous positions, which is why she does a protection ceremony before each investigation.

This brings us to a subject that I'm still a bit fuzzy on, despite repeated attempts by Rona to explain it to me. Can these beings hurt you? That's my question. Rona says no, but at the same time, she does protection ceremonies and tells me that spirits can interact with our physical world. At one point, she told me that one of her spirit guides smacked her in the head to tell her to get writing instead of just talking about writing. That seems like a sort of aggressive-cheerleader-y thing to do, but coming with good intentions. Still, if a ghost can smack you in the head without the intent to harm, couldn't they do it *with* the intent to harm?

"No," Rona said emphatically when I asked her about that. "They can't hurt you. They can't."

Speaking about the spirit guide who smacked her and made her forehead turn red, Rona speculated it might be similar to psychosomatic illness. "You know how somebody can make themselves sick because they are worrying? This is almost the same thing…. I mean, how do I know that it's not like an internal thing, where she came into my mind and it seemed like she smacked me and my forehead went red?"

Recalling for a moment that I don't really believe in spirits and I do believe in psychosomatic illness, this seems a very logical explanation to me. However, if you do believe in spirits, and believe they have the power to cause things like that, why would you not believe they could use that power for ill?

Rona's answer, which doesn't really satisfy me, was, "We don't believe in demons, and we don't believe in devils … it's all human; it's all negative humans that cause a lot of this stuff."

I share all this to say that when Rona and Stephanie went down that hallway in the Charles Camsell Hospital and ventured into one of the offices, they both very quickly began to feel ill and did not linger. "I wasn't scared," Rona said. But she could feel a deep negative energy. "The person who either had occupied that office when they were alive, or decided to occupy it after they were dead, was a really nasty, nasty person."

Their investigation concluded, Ben and Rona had a celebratory shot from the bottle of Crown Royal that had been their admission fee into the hospital. Then, while Ben took Stephanie home, Darin drove Rona back to his place.

Once they arrived at Darin's apartment, he and Rona had a drink together to celebrate a successful investigation. After she finished, Rona excused herself to go to the washroom. That is the last thing she remembers from that night.

When Ben arrived at the apartment sometime later, Darin told him Rona had gone into the bathroom quite a while ago and he hadn't heard from her since. He told Ben that she wasn't responding when he knocked on the door, and that he was quite concerned about her.

Deciding to put her safety over her modesty, Ben and Darin opened the bathroom door to find Rona lying on the floor. She was sound asleep but scratching at her arms just like the spirit from the psych ward had scratched at hers. No matter what they did, Ben and Darin couldn't wake her up, so they covered her with a blanket and left her to wake in her own time.

Rona wasn't the only one whose sleep was unusual that night. Every single person who had been on the investigation slept poorly, and the next day they were all exhausted beyond what could easily be explained away as sleep deprivation. What's more, many of them had disturbing but non-specific nightmares for weeks afterward.

Rona tells me that using drugs or alcohol can open you up to the presence and influence of spirits. She believes the small amount of drinking they did on site and at Darin's place afterward, combined with the fact that their pre-investigation protection ceremony was interrupted and they didn't do a protection ceremony before leaving the hospital, may have left their group uncomfortably receptive to the spirits.

Whatever the cause, and despite my skepticism of all things supernatural, the storyteller part of me really wants to believe that Rona provided the way out for that poor girl on the psych ward. And maybe, now that she's free of the hospital, she can find peace.

Speaking of finding peace: in response to the rumours and beliefs that Indigenous spirits might be trapped in the Camsell, developer Gene Dub recently spoke at a symposium about the hospital and said once the asbestos is removed from the building, he would welcome an Indigenous Elder to come in and perform a healing ceremony. Whether you believe that will put spirits to rest or not, it will definitely help put some minds at rest, at the very least.

Connecting the Dots

This hospital's troubled history and the long amount of time it has stood empty have both really fuelled the imaginations of the surrounding community, not to mention those of everyone whose lives it has touched. Skeptical me is pretty sure those two elements combined could more than explain the great bulk of reportedly paranormal happenings attributed to the building.

For example, there's a Facebook group, "I'm obsessed with the Charles Camsell Hospital" that, as of October 2018, has just more than 1,100 members.

A few months ago, the construction workers at the Camsell hung what are essentially reflective balloons designed to resemble owls in a couple of the hospital windows. The idea was that they would scare other birds away. It didn't seem to work and they took them down a couple of weeks later. However, during the time they were in the window, I saw them featured in a couple of photo posts on the Facebook group, casting them in the role of ghosts. The photos were all taken at night, when it would be difficult to tell what the subject matter was; the balloons were head shaped, moved about in even the slightest breeze, and reflected light back, like eyes. They were designed to look alive to scare other birds away, but to nighttime visitors with good imaginations that had already been primed to expect ghosts, that is what they looked like.

As for the room covered with blood, which disturbed some explorers within the hospital, I suggest that if it were real blood, it would long ago have faded or been eliminated by the elements. However, *Whitecoats*, the medical comedy movie, featured lots of blood and gory special effects. According to a March 7, 2003, *Edmonton Sun* article about the filming of the movie, special-effects expert Dan Rebert was hired to provide "fake blood, prosthetic limbs and internal organs. Lots and lots of organs." Given that, I suspect the bloodied room people have seen is more likely an old movie set than the scene of something more gruesome.

That being said, I can't explain away everything people have experienced at the Camsell. The elevator that moved without power, for example, or people hearing impossible voices over radios. And given the hospital's past, I believe that if anywhere was going to be haunted, the Camsell would be the place.

In April 2016, a symposium was held to explore the stories of the Camsell. After the symposium was complete, it became apparent that more discussion was needed, so the Edmonton Heritage Council partnered with Mtset Productions to make a short documentary about the hospital. That film, which is accessible on the Edmonton Heritage Council's website, packed a lot into thirteen minutes.

"It's such an interesting way to look at this building," Gene Dub said. "How it has been helpful to people and helped them live, while on the other hand it contributed to the demise of some of their culture." He went on to say that perhaps some of the delays he's encountered in developing this site were a bit of a blessing in disguise, because they gave him time to really learn about the history of the building and adjust the development plan to take those things and the Truth and Reconciliation movement into account. "And we will do something toward that end. Which we wouldn't have done had it been developed five, ten years ago."

I want to give the last word in this section to two Indigenous women who appear in the video: Mini Aodla Freeman, an Inuit woman who worked as a government translator and was frequently sent to the Charles Camsell to work; and Debbie Coulter, a Métis woman who was a patient at the hospital in 1985.

"I think it's important for the souls of the people who died here, and in honour of the memory of those who served and did good things here, I'd like to keep that memory going as well," Debbie says. "So it's not just a bad place; there was also some good that came out of here. Yeah. Keep that balance."

Later on in the documentary, Mini looks around the gutted Camsell, but perhaps she is speaking of more than just the physical structure when she says, "Yes. They have a lot of work to do here."

11

Dominion Hotel Building — 10324 82 Avenue NW

History

The Dominion Hotel Building, built in 1903, features a gorgeous, ornate facade that fronts a relatively plain three-storey brick building. The facade, which includes intricately decorated wooden balconies in the chinoiserie style and a decorative central cupola, gives the building a classically Victorian appearance. It was the fanciest building on 82 Avenue (again, this is also known as Whyte Avenue) at the time of its construction.

Built by Robert McKernan, an early settler, the building was originally a hotel. The ground floor consisted of a lobby, a dining room, and a beer parlour. The building was also, according to Nadine Bailey of Edmonton Ghost Tours, Edmonton's first brothel. Legend says that upon learning of the brothel's existence, men lined up around the block, waiting for their turn to avail themselves of the services offered. However, when the local women's association learned about the goings-on at the Dominion Hotel, they stormed in and threw all the prostitutes' worldly belongings

The Dominion Hotel Building, built in 1903, has a very distinctive look, an interesting history, and possibly some visitors from beyond the grave.

out the window into the road and then chased the women all the way across the river.*

When Prohibition came along in 1916, the building ceased to function as a hotel; instead, the upper floors were converted into rental apartments and the ground floor became home to many different retailers.

The building was declared a historic resource in 1976, and in the 1980s the facade was completely restored and the rest of the building almost entirely reconstructed. It was scheduled to undergo a very similar process in 2018, so by the time this book goes to print, it could be boasting a completely different interior. And if, as Rona says, ghosts are stirred up by renovations, perhaps there will be new stories to tell by then as well.

What We Knew Going In

I didn't know anything about the Dominion Hotel Building before I started work on this book. However, Rona, who used to give ghost tours around Edmonton, was well acquainted with it, as the building was one of the highlights on the tour. So, she had researched its history long before this book was conceived. Later, after she had stopped giving historical tours, Rona and Ben used the Two Rooms restaurant, which was located in the building for a time, to host "Ghost Dinners." People would come, eat, hear a presentation about the paranormal, and hopefully spot a ghost ... or at least experience something eerie.

Encounters

At the Ghost Dinners, there were cameras and monitors set up so that everyone in the dining room enjoying their dinner could watch the screens and see what the cameras were capturing, both in the room where they were eating and also in other parts of the restaurant. Those

---

* edmontonjournal.com/entertainment/local-arts/old-strathconas-haunted-past-continues-to-draw-crowds-to-ghost-tour

cameras caught a lot of spirit orbs, including some that were rushing right at people. If the people eating saw an orb headed for them on the monitor, they would duck out of its way.

What would happen, I asked Rona, if they didn't duck and got struck by one of those orbs?

"Well, you wouldn't. You're just looking at the TV and thinking 'this thing is coming near me,'" she said, explaining why people were ducking. "I think if it did hit you and went through you, you'd sort of feel a little bit of a coldness or a jelly substance kind of thing, but it wouldn't be bad and it wouldn't hurt you in any way."

It didn't surprise Rona that they were getting a lot of activity on the cameras, because there were renovations going on upstairs and renovations tend to stir up spirits. It did surprise her, in a pleasant way, when one of the men working upstairs came down and said, "What are you guys doing down here?" When the restaurant owner explained about the Ghost Dinners, he nodded and said, "Oh, that makes sense now."

It seems that a lot of odd little things were going on upstairs — things moving around, glasses clinking when no one was clinking them, that sort of thing. Based on that, Rona took the whole group upstairs to see what they could see. Unfortunately, they didn't see much. Perhaps some more orbs and the like, but there was no climactic encounter like you might expect in a horror movie or scary story.

At least not right then.

As part of their audiovisual set-up, Ben and Rona had one camera pointed at the door, so it was also capturing people who were walking by on busy Whyte Avenue.

That camera caught someone walking very oddly. When Rona demonstrated how they moved to me, it was very much like how the woman emerges from the television in the movie *The Ring*. If you've seen that scene, you know exactly what I'm talking about. If you haven't … it's sort of like there's a glitch affecting your body so that you can't move normally. Everything looks painful and herky-jerky. Definitely not right.

The person glitched their way down the street until they reached a blind spot where none of the cameras could see them. And then, when they reappeared on the cameras, it wasn't the same person. Another person had taken their place and continued to walk by, perfectly normally.

What happened in that blind spot? Man, I wish we knew….

Connecting the Dots

To me, the most interesting ghost story to come out of the Dominion Hotel Building is that of the person glitching down the street outside, who transforms into a completely different person after entering a blind spot. Unfortunately, although I looked, I couldn't find any events in the history of this building that might be used to explain a broken ghost. Assuming it was a ghost. Even if it was, because whatever it was Rona saw was actually outside the building, on the street, it's possible that it is not associated with the Dominion Hotel Building at all.

12

The Guilty Martini — 10338 81 Avenue

History

According to Rona's research, at one time this property housed W.J. Scott and Son Carriage Builders. At that time, they worked on the ground floor and lived on the top floor. After they left, the structure was used as an apartment building for some time before hosting a succession of different businesses.

What We Knew Going In

I never went to the Guilty Martini (or any business located in the building that housed the Guilty Martini, which is no longer in business). The first time I heard about it was when I was talking to Rona and Ben about the Charles Camsell. At that time, the Guilty Martini came up in passing because they had done an investigation there the day after they visited the Camsell and were still reeling a bit from its effects.

Rona had been familiar with the Guilty Martini before her investigations, and was friends with its manager. She had performed several official investigations of it over the years and also occasionally visited as a patron. So, she wasn't going into her investigations without knowing anything; and because she had done a number of investigations at the site, there was a cumulative depth to her research, something not present in her work at other sites.

Encounters

There were two dominant entities that haunted (keep reading to find out why I used the past tense there) the Guilty Martini. The first was a male spirit whom visitors had named Dapper Dan, and the second was the thing in the staircase. We'll begin with Dapper Dan.

The Guilty Martini had two floors, and the top level had a railing that would let people look down safely at the dance floor on the main level. One evening, when Rona was sitting on the main level, she looked up and just happened to see Dapper Dan standing at the railing and looking down at her. "He looked like he had some mischief in his eyes," she said. "Which is stupid, because I couldn't really see his eyes, but I just knew he was a very mischievous spirit."

Rona's second impression of Dapper Dan was that he had been very aptly named. "He was dressed in a very nice brown suit, brown pants. He had a bowler-type hat on and a moustache," she told me. "He was, indeed, a very dapper-looking man."

Dan was a dominant spirit, and there were frequently two other submissive spirits who hung around with him. Both of them were women, and it was Rona's impression that in life there had been a love triangle of some sort between the three. She thought that something about that love triangle had left them stuck in our realm, unable to move on after death. She didn't know what it was exactly that they needed to resolve, but because they hadn't, they were stuck at the Guilty Martini.

Things weren't all hunky-dory for the ghostly trio even in death, however. During one of her investigations, Rona captured an electronic voice phenomenon (EVP) of the three of them having a huge argument in the upstairs stairwell. She couldn't make out any specific words they were screaming at each other, but she says the fight was really, really noisy. Whatever had them all riled up had reduced them to a screaming cacophony of anger.

Rona doesn't think that Dapper Dan was a big fan of the loud music and copious amounts of alcohol accompanying the nightclub scene that was the Guilty Martini. It seems that his displeasure with the atmosphere of the club may have spurred him to action; many of the things he was accused of committing could easily be interpreted as minor acts of sabotage. For example, when the servers and bartenders were setting up before their shift, they would frequently hear glasses and bottles clink together, although none of the glasses and bottles around them had moved. Such things could be unsettling. Phantom sounds, coming from a phantom source, and then there were the footsteps they'd hear when the bar was still closed and they should have been alone in the building. Many people reported hearing the sound of someone walking up and down the stairs or walking around upstairs, but when they went to see who it was, there wasn't anyone there.

Sometimes when the servers came to work in the morning, they'd find that the tables they'd prepped late the previous night, at the end of their shift, had been sabotaged. The little "specials cards" and ashtrays they'd carefully placed on each table the night before would be knocked over onto the floor, and bottles behind the bar would have been moved from their rightful locations into random places.

Dan especially seemed to like to scare the women who worked at the bar — the male employees had far fewer stories than the women did. Women would frequently catch a glimpse of the shadowy shape of a man out of the corner of their eye, but when they turned to face it directly, it would vanish. And one time, very late at night, the club manager thought she was alone in the building, but when she went to use the washroom, the stall door suddenly slammed shut on her — as though moved by an invisible hand.

Speaking of hands? Another time, a waitress was just minding her own business when suddenly a man's arm burst through the cigarette machine and tried to grab her.

In addition to the EVP that showed Dan arguing with his girl-friends, Rona also captured another EVP of him saying, "That's my favourite kind of vodka." Unfortunately, there were several different types of vodka nearby at the time, so it's impossible to know which particular brand he favoured.

Dan wasn't the only dominant spirit at the Guilty Martini. He was the most benign one, however. The other dominant spirit Rona encountered was the one she dubbed "the thing in the stairwell," and it was far more menacing and messed up than Dan.

The stairwell in question went from the west end of the upstairs lounge up to the roof of the building. People frequently reported feeling unsettled or even fearful when they went near the stairwell, and some people who entered the stairwell area said they felt as though someone had touched or pushed them, even though they were alone in the space.

One day, the very heavy door at the top of the stairwell opened and slammed shut again, seemingly of its own accord. Rona wasn't sure how to interpret that occurrence — was it a warning that they should leave, or just the ghost letting them know it was there? She couldn't be sure, but it was definitely not friendly or well intentioned.

The spirit itself was what Rona calls a fractured spirit. "A fractured spirit," Rona explained, "is a spirit who has done some extremely negative things in their life. Things like murder, domestic abuse, stuff like that. And what happens when they pass is, sometimes, some of the victim residue or things they have done kind of stick to them. They don't look like a fully formed human spirit. So, this thing in the stairwell. I had picked up on that he had been, at one time, a young man, and for some reason they were keeping animals on the roof — mainly birds or rabbits — and one day he just lost it over I don't know what and went up with a baseball bat or something and battered the animals to death in their cages."

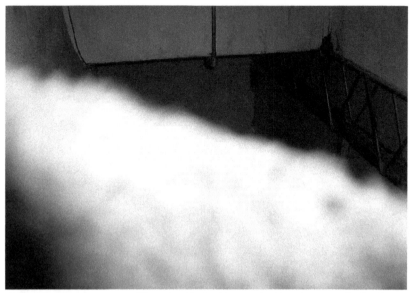

"The thing in the stairwell" at the Guilty Martini. In this photograph, the fractured spirit takes the form of a "huge, cloudy vortex."

As a result of his actions, his spirit was fractured, and the residue of those animal victims stuck to him when he passed. So, he no longer appeared human. Rather, Rona said, "He looked like Pig Pen from Charlie Brown, but with beaks and ears and different things sticking out of him."

Rona actually captured a photograph of the thing in the stairwell. In the picture, it doesn't look like how Rona saw it, but rather like a cloud. But inside. It's quite weird.

Rona was ascending the staircase to the roof when one of the people behind her said, "Rona, behind you!" She quickly turned around and took a series of photographs. In the first and third photos, there was nothing unusual — just a staircase — but in the second picture, there was what Rona described as a "huge, cloudy vortex" that was moving across the stairwell. People have looked at the picture and thought it was just smoke, but Rona said no. "How the hell did a big cloud of smoke just appear in the stairwell?" she asked. There was no wind, nothing that could explain it.

The fractured spirit isn't the only one that inhabited the staircase at the Guilty Martini. This orb was photographed there as well.

The owner of the Guilty Martini was stabbed outside his bar one Canada Day. He survived. Rona does not suggest that he haunts the space, but she wonders if the thing in the stairwell was extending its influence — fearful, rageful, fragmented — out into the area around the nightclub. She says it seemed like, around the time the stabbing occurred, there was a lot of aggression in that area, and her partner,

Ben, who was a friend of the owner, said that for a time there were frequently fights and stabbings nearby.

I can't help but wonder: if the spirit in the stairwell was influencing people's emotions, could it be influencing its fellow spirits as well? After all, the argument between Dapper Dan and his girlfriends that Rona recorded took place in that stairwell. Perhaps they weren't immune to their roommate's aura.

I've referred to all the spirits haunting the Guilty Martini in the past tense because Rona moved on the spirits that had been lingering there. All four of them, even the thing in the stairwell. So that property is no longer haunted, and the fractured spirit in particular can no longer spread its negativity.

Connecting the Dots

I'm not sure there are any meaningful dots to connect for this one. We have no way of knowing whether any of the spirits were actually connected in life to this building or if they just sort of ended up there after their deaths. Even if they were directly connected to the building in life, it would be nearly impossible, given the information that we have — a well-dressed dude who likes vodka and women, and an angry young man who killed domestic animals — to identify conclusively who the spirits were in life. And the actual building doesn't seem to have any historically significant events tied to it.

The identity of Dapper Dan, his girlfriends, and the thing in the stairwell will have to remain a mystery.

– 13 –

Garneau Theatre — 8712 109 Street NW

History

Designated a historic building in 2009, the Garneau Theatre is the only surviving modernist theatre still operating in Alberta. It was designed by renowned Alberta architect William George Blakey, and opened on October 24, 1940.

Little expense was spared on the theatre's construction, and some creativity went into its decoration. For example, on opening night, the foyer sported furniture that had originally been commissioned for the visit of the king and queen of England a few years prior. The owner, Bill Wilson, arranged to borrow it from Eaton's, where it had been on display. This meant that on opening night, visitors could actually sit in the same seat royalty had, just a few years before. That alone was quite an incentive for people to attend.

Apparently, the furniture was never returned to Eaton's and ended up in Bill's house.

Much to Rona's disappointment, it turns out that there are no Prohibition tunnels associated with the building. However,

The facade of the Garneau Theatre at night. Rumours abound about hauntings in this historic theatre, but there are very few first-hand accounts.

according to a tour guide, there is "a massive David Lynch–style industrial fan on the roof and one on the back of the building." These are part of the heating and cooling system for the theatre and there is a huge tunnel — big enough to crawl through — that connects them. Perhaps they are the source of the urban legend regarding the Prohibition-era tunnels beneath the theatre? It's difficult to say.

These days, the Metro Cinema Society controls the Garneau Theatre. In addition to continuing to show movies there, the society also rents the location out for private events.

What We Knew Going In

The Garneau Theatre is interesting because what we knew going in turned out to be untrue.

Before we visited the Garneau, Rona had learned about the Prohibition-era tunnels from a reliable source. She'd hoped to find out more about them, and further wondered if there might be any spirit activity associated with them. I had no background information about the theatre. I'd attended the theatre as a patron a time or two but hadn't heard any fun stories about ghosts, or even tunnels.

Encounters

Rona and I, along with several members of my family, took a backstage tour of the Garneau on October 28, 2018. Based on the marketing and timing of the event, we expected to be taking a ghost tour. It turned out that was not the case. In fact, once the whole group was assembled, one of the very first things our tour guide said was, "This is not a ghost tour." To be fair to us, the tour was right before Halloween, was advertised alongside actual ghost tours and haunted houses, was called "the Garneau Ghost Light Tour," and promised, in part, a tour of backstage "haunts." To be fair to the tour, they never once said it was a ghost tour. We just assumed.

The ghost light tour gave us a detailed overview of the complete history of the theatre and several of the people associated with it. For any history buffs who find themselves in Edmonton, I definitely recommend it, because I am going to hit on only some of the highlights of this beautiful building's history.

Anyway. The five of us showed up expecting a ghost tour and ghost stories and were almost immediately informed that was absolutely not going to happen. Still, we were there. We were committed. So we stuck around.

And I'm glad we did. Our tour guide, Dave Clarke, was engaging and entertaining, and he obviously feels very strongly about the Garneau and loves sharing its history with people. It was fun to clomp

Ghost lights are left on when the theatre is otherwise dark. Practically, they light the stage to prevent accidents, but superstition says they also allow for theatre ghosts to perform on stage.

around as a group, up onto the stage with the ghost light from which the tour takes its name, out into the back alley, to the front of the theatre to admire its architectural detail, downstairs to the art deco apartment secreted away in the basement, and even up into the projectionist's room.

While we were up on stage and our host was talking about the ghost light, Dave explained that it serves a practical purpose — it helps ensure that the first person in the theatre in the morning can see well enough not to fall off the edge of the stage — and also a superstitious one. It's left on overnight for the ghosts.

"Are there ghosts in this building?" he asked. "I don't know. Maybe?"

According to Rona, the answer to that question is actually "Yes. Sometimes."

After we finished the tour, I turned to Rona and said, "Well, what did you think? Did you see anything?" and was happily surprised when she said yes.

While we were up in the projectionist's room, most of us on the tour were listening to the projectionist talk and looking down at the red curtain drawn across the screen (and Vincent Price's face, which was being projected onto it), but Rona was seeing something else. Something none of the rest of us could see. She saw a ghost in the audience.

Rona saw the spirit of a woman wearing dark clothing and bangles from her wrist to her elbow on both arms. The ghost turned toward Rona and saw her watching, then bent at the waist and scooted backward out of the room. There was another detail that fascinated me. As the ghost looked at Rona, the complexion of her face kept changing from dark to light and back to dark again. When I asked Rona about that, she said, "I don't know what she was trying to show me with that. Perhaps that she was mixed race? I'm not sure."

Rona didn't think the spirit was a resident of the theatre. She thought it was more likely that she came and went — possibly related to the movies showing at any given time. Because why shouldn't a ghost time their trips to the theatre based on what is showing? We do.

Connecting the Dots

Rona believes that the ghost she saw in the audience was only a visitor, not a resident, so there is no reason to believe she has any connection to the building or its history at all. Whatever the case, it's possible that if she comes by from time to time just to watch the movies, other ghosts do, too. So, while you're watching that scary flick at the Garneau, you can't be sure that the empty-looking seat next to you actually is.

- 14 -

Wee Book Inn — 10310 82 Avenue NW

History

The Wee Book Inn is a small chain of second-hand bookstores in Edmonton. Many stores have come and gone in the chain over the nearly fifty years since the first store opened, but we are going to focus only on the original Whyte (82) Avenue location.

The chain's founder, Darwin Luxford, opened the first store on Whyte Avenue in 1971. It was a very small shop, only about seven feet wide and thirty feet deep, which is why it was called the "Wee" Book Inn. The shop was so popular that within months Luxford was negotiating to get more space from the building next door. After a few years, he actually built a new, two-storey building on Whyte Avenue to accommodate the store's growing customer base and to allow for a larger variety of books.

Sadly, in December 1990 a fire devastated the Whyte Avenue location (compounding the loss, a second fire also destroyed the north-side location in that same month). The building was so damaged that it could not be repaired and was torn down. Construction

The Wee Book Inn on Whyte Avenue is, as its name suggests, a rather small space crammed full of two floors of books. And possibly a ghost or two.

began on a new building in August 1991 and eight months later, the Whyte Avenue location of the Wee Book Inn reopened.

A side note: Each Wee Book Inn location shares an endearing feature — it always has a shop cat. At the time of this writing, the Whyte Avenue location is presided over by a fluffy beauty named Fleur.

What We Knew Going In

I have been to the Wee Book Inn on Whyte Avenue several times. On the surface, it is a rather typical used bookstore, but the second floor has several lovely (and locked) cases containing the more expensive books — first editions, rare versions, that sort of thing. I don't know anything about its history, and neither does Rona. Like me, Rona has also visited the Wee Book Inn, but never in any official investigatory capacity.

Encounters

Although Rona has never done a formal investigation of the bookstore, the upstairs space is such a quiet little oasis that she's been able to pick up on a couple of spirits up there without even trying.

The first spirit she encountered was that of a little girl. Rona got only the briefest of glimpses of her, however, because the girl's favourite hobby is hiding in and around the bookshelves and only peeking out to spy on all the people coming and going.

When Rona returned some time later, the girl wasn't there, but a different spirit was. Rona sensed the spirit of an old man, but she never saw him. When she described him to me, I was reminded of Giles from *Buffy the Vampire Slayer* — a slightly stodgy man who really loves books and might be a bit set in his ways. "He's very overprotective of the older books," Rona said. But because they are largely locked up, I think he probably needn't worry.

Rona wasn't able to get a sense of whether either of the spirits was a perpetual guest of the bookstore or if they just sort of came and went as their whims dictated. They were clearly very comfortable in the space, but so would most people be.

Connecting the Dots

Given Rona's description of the spirits haunting the upstairs of the Wee Book Inn, I can see no reason to assume they are in any way attached to the history of the shop. The bookstore's founder, Darwin

Luxford, passed away in 2014 at the age of seventy-one. He might, I suppose, feel overly protective of the rare books and want to hang about to keep an eye on things, but all the reports I read about him describe him as a very social and friendly person who loved to meet and interact with people. It doesn't seem to me that someone with that personality would lurk upstairs in the quietest part of the bookstore; nor would he be so shy that Rona couldn't catch a glimpse of him. Perhaps the Wee Book Inn is just inhabited by a little girl who likes quiet people-watching, and a dude who really likes old books. I mean, if I got to pick where I would haunt or visit after my death, a bookstore would not be at the bottom of the list.

– 15 –

Mount Pleasant Cemetery — 5420 106 Street NW

History

This cemetery sits on one of the highest points of land in the whole city, which allows for beautiful views of its surroundings. Although when the cemetery was established, it was well outside the boundaries of the city, today the city has not only expanded to reach it, but has completely surrounded it. The cemetery now exists as a quiet green space surrounded on all sides by developments.

Burials on this beautiful parcel of land began in the 1880s, and although it has been expanded several times, it is now full. The costs of upkeeping the cemetery have been an ongoing problem, and in researching this piece, I've discovered stories of debt, perpetual care fees, and tax bills, none of which are of much interest to this writer. There are some fascinating stories, though, as the cemetery contains the graves of some notable and interesting people, including one man whose name has come up again and again in this book: Alexander Cameron Rutherford (1857–1941).

What We Knew Going In

Rona had never done an official investigation at Mount Pleasant Cemetery, nor had she researched its history. She had visited it, however, which put her a step ahead of me. I've never been there, but I did enjoy looking at some of the many photographs of it. The photographs show it to be a beautifully maintained cemetery, with some gently rolling hills, a tranquil-looking indoor niche building (a structure filled with niches inset into the walls to contain the final remains of those who have been cremated), and several columbaria, which also hold urns containing cremains; i.e., the ashes of someone who has been cremated. It looks to me like it might be one of the most peaceful locations you'll find within Edmonton city limits.

Encounters

There's something you need to know about Rona: she owns a hearse. Yup. A hearse. It's not the car she drives to run to the store, but when she talks about it, you can see the pride shining in her eyes. She also belongs to a hearse club. Because *of course* there is a hearse club.

Every year, St. Albert (a small city just outside Edmonton) has a week full of events, "Rock'n August," to raise money to support diabetes research. One of the biggest parts of that weeklong event is a car show, in which Rona's hearse club participated on one occasion. On the last day of Rock'n August, it was tradition at the time for all of them to get into their hearses and drive together, convoy style, to the Mount Pleasant Cemetery.

It was at the conclusion of this drive that Rona encountered a spirit in the cemetery. She and some of her fellow hearse owners were taking pictures of the grounds, and of their cars in the grounds (what better place to photograph a hearse, after all?). Rona was offering them suggestions as to how to maximize their chances of capturing evidence of paranormal activity in their photos. While Rona was chatting with a father and his adult son who were having mixed results with their photographs, a couple of ladies strayed a bit away from the group. They were looking at the grave markers and chatting together when Rona looked up and spotted something.

Just off to the side, not very far from the women, was a spirit. It was a "shadow person" — a spirit in human form but without any features or details — and it was slowly crawling along the ground toward the women. Rona watched it for a little while and then said, "You guys, I just wanted you to know that there's a creepy spirit crawling on the ground toward you and I don't know if you want to move or if you want to stay where you are and see what happens ..."

She hadn't even finished her sentence before the women bolted away. Much to Rona's disappointment. Even when she told me the story later, you could hear it in her voice: a sort of wistful note, thinking about what might have been. "I wanted them to stay there because I wanted to see, well, what's he going to do? It's not like he could do anything."

Rona still doesn't know what the ghost was planning to do when it reached those women, but she did add, "Some of the spirits in cemeteries are silly. They really are. They're just goofs."

I suppose if I had to spend day in and day out in a cemetery — possibly the very same one where my body was rotting — it might make me a bit goofy, too.

Connecting the Dots

I'm not sure there are any dots to connect here. Because the spirit Rona saw was a shadow person, we don't know anything about it at all, except perhaps that it's either a bit of a goofball, or just downright creepy. And we don't need to know the cemetery's history to figure that out. We don't even know that the spirit spotted in the graveyard was actually buried in the graveyard. Certainly, ghosts don't need a reason to haunt graveyards, of all places — although if I were going to pick a place to haunt after death, it would not be anywhere near my physical body.

Thinking out loud, I commented that while cemeteries are peaceful and all, I couldn't help but think they would get boring after a time.

Rona pointed out that we have no way of knowing what the ghosts are seeing. When we look at a cemetery, we see a field of gravestones stretching off into the distance, but spirits exist in another dimension, so who knows what they see. A cemetery for us could be a tropical oasis or a happenin' rave for them.

"I don't know," Rona said. "It's beyond my comprehension, it really is. But I know that all this ties into quantum physics, and one day I would just love for us to say, 'Well, if we can see neutrons and we can see atoms and all these other particles, then why can't we see spirits?'"

Of course, this observation can be used by either side of the skeptical divide, so I'm not going to go into it in any more depth here. I will say, however, that I'd be really curious to know what spirits see when they look at graveyards. Someone should ask them.

- 16 -

Edmonton Cemetery — 11820 107 Avenue NW

History

Much like Mount Pleasant Cemetery, this cemetery began its existence on the very edge of town. Now, however, it's not very far from downtown and is, in fact, bisected by a very busy road. It contains the Military Field of Honour, where soldiers' graves are laid out with no distinction for rank — officers rest alongside enlisted men. This Military Field of Honour was established in 1922, and even now, when on occasion I've taken a shortcut through the cemetery, I have seen flowers on the graves.

Many notable Edmonton settlers and people from the past are buried here, including Emily Murphy of the "Famous Five."

What We Knew Going In

I live relatively near this cemetery, and it's even closer to the school where my daughter danced for years, so I've walked by and even through it from time to time. Rona and I never visited this location together, but before the visit I will be writing about in this section, she hadn't done any research or previously investigated it.

Corvids are sometimes thought to be messengers between worlds. Perhaps that's why this old guy was spotted hanging out in the cemetery.

Encounters

"Hey, you!" the burly male spirit barked at Rona. "Yeah. You. What are you doing here?"

Mike — which, as Rona came to learn, was his name — was a spirit who inhabited the Edmonton Cemetery with two other, weaker, female spirits. He had a military-type bearing. He was definitely not going to be pushed around and was very much in charge of all he surveyed. He saw himself as a bit of a caretaker and didn't like too many people in the cemetery at one time, so Rona's little group had attracted his attention. And not really in a good way. He was aggressive and made it clear he wasn't going to be okay with any vandalism or that sort of thing going on in *his* cemetery.

Rona patiently explained their purpose for being there. She told him they weren't there to desecrate anything, but to take pictures and learn more if they could. "I'm here because I'm so interested in spirits like you because you're not in your body anymore, you're in

A tomb in the Edmonton Cemetery.

a different formation now," she told him. "So I'd just really love to get to know you and take some pictures of you."

After she explained the group's purpose to him, he was much more welcoming of them and chilled right out.

At one point, Rona asked if she could take a photograph of him and he said sort of mockingly, "You already have." Rona scrolled through the pictures on her digital camera and, sure enough, there was a photo of a really strong, solid-looking orange beam coming up out of the ground, flanked by two weaker striated beams also emerging from the ground.

The strong beam in the centre is presumably Mike, and the two fainter beams would be the women. Mike, Rona tells me, is the dominant spirit at the cemetery and the two women are submissive to him.

Rona never really got a strong sense of the women there, but one of the people who was at the cemetery with her, a woman with psychic abilities somewhat different from Rona's, said that she got a stronger feeling for them. Even she couldn't make out any details about them, though. Only that they were female, and not as strong as Mike.

Connecting the Dots

As with the Mount Pleasant Cemetery, I'm not sure there are actually any dots to be connected here. These three spirits enjoy hanging out at Edmonton Cemetery, but that doesn't mean they are necessarily connected to it. Given the fact that there are a lot of military graves at the cemetery and Mike gave the impression of coming from a military background, it's possible he has a connection to the place, but we can't say for sure.

- 17 -

The Granite Club — 8620 107 Street NW

History

Officially opened for curling on December 20, 1920, the Granite Curling Club is one of the oldest clubs of its kind in Alberta. Ever since it opened, it has been an important part of the city's curling community and, according to the history reported on its website, has truly been a groundbreaker inside the city and beyond. For example, it was the first rink to sport the coloured rings that are now the game's trademark, and also the first in Edmonton to have artificial ice.

The Granite Club has hosted a fair number of large, important events and bonspiels, including Canadian and provincial championships. An overwhelming number of its online reviews are incredibly positive. People love the space, and the atmosphere, the people, the food, and the ice.

What We Knew Going In

I had never heard of the Granite Club before I began work on this book. Rona and Ben, however, had spent a fair amount of time in it after hours because it was one of the buildings they had a contract to clean back in their days of doing commercial cleaning.

Encounters

Rona didn't do an official investigation of this building, but because she had spent a lot of time there during quiet hours, she had a good sense of the spirits that frequent it. Her favourite was a gentleman she calls a "caretaker" spirit. He hangs around the bar on the second floor. He sounds like a jovial sort, judging from the way Rona describes him. She doesn't think he moves around much, preferring to stick close to his bar upstairs, where he can still watch the curling while making sure everyone is having a good time.

There were two other spirits she speaks of far less fondly, however. Two she'd felt following her around while she was cleaning. Rona describes them as very negative and malicious. The sort of men with bad intentions who like to pair up to commit violent crimes against women. Rona sounds exceptionally confident of the fact that not only do they still contemplate that sort of thing as spirits, but they committed such acts together when they were alive. Kidnapping, raping, and murdering women — or some combination of those things.

On several occasions when she was trying to work, she could feel them there, constantly there, looming over her with their dark intentions. And of course they could tell they were unnerving her, which just made them gleeful and emboldened them more. She tried to ignore them — I'm sure that's a scenario plenty of people can relate to: trying to ignore the people who are harassing you — but it just didn't work. They were still there. Still looming. Still leering.

"I had to clean the bathrooms," Rona said with a sigh, "and I knew as soon as I went into the bathroom, they'd be right behind me."

She knew they couldn't hurt her, but she'd had enough. Enough of them following her around and making her uncomfortable.

"And I thought, 'ya know, I'm just going to send them into the light,'" she says. "And I did."

She says it like it's an everyday thing, and I guess for Rona it is, but imagine being able to say, "You know what? I've about had enough of you, ghostie; into the light with you!" I love that image (although I suppose if everyone could do that, it would definitely not be good for the horror genre). Another thing I love about Rona sending these particular spirits into the light is that she says they were shocked by it. Shocked! How could a woman possibly have the power, the ability, to send them away like that? I love the idea that two dudes who preyed on women in life and enjoyed it so much they continued after they died were beaten by one exasperated woman who had had enough and just wanted to clean the bathrooms in peace, thank you very much.

Rona told me this story while we were sitting by the window in Remedy Café on 124 Street. The sun was streaming in. I had a chai latte cupped between my hands. Life was good. But as she spoke about these dark men and their darker intentions, I was a little discomforted to see wings fluttering over my chai. After a moment's confusion, however, I realized the moth wasn't in my drink. It wasn't even in the restaurant. It was just outside the window. It was black — you don't see a lot of black moths around here, so that stuck out for me — and it flitted around the window while Rona talked and then, at the conclusion of her story, when she spoke about casting the spirits into the light, the moth flitted away.

Coincidence, I'm sure. But one that makes for a good story.

Connecting the Dots

I was unable to discover a single eerie or unsettling thing in the club's history. That doesn't mean they don't exist — lots of things happen that I might not stumble across in my research, but I couldn't find anything. It's my feeling that the spirits Rona encountered in the bathrooms (and subsequently sent into the light) were not at all connected to the club in life, but just happened upon the building afterward. The good news is that, either way, they aren't there anymore.

– 18 –

Edmonton 1881 School — 10425 99 Avenue

History

The Edmonton 1881 schoolhouse was the very first school built in Edmonton. When it was erected, it was the first sawn-lumber building in Edmonton. It had six windows, which boasted the largest panes of glass in the community at that time. Built in 1881, it actually opened as a school in January of 1882. It functioned as a school (and occasionally a meeting hall or courthouse) from that time until 1904. Shortly before the First World War, the school was moved from its original location and turned into a private residence. However, in 1982 it was returned to its original site behind McKay Avenue School and extensively renovated to restore it to something resembling its original appearance. It is, according to the registry of Canada's historic places, Alberta's oldest extant school building.

What We Knew Going In

People don't whisper about the McKay Avenue School being haunted; they speak about it in full voices, casually, as though it is an accepted

The McKay Avenue School Archives and Museum is purportedly haunted. Rona knows for sure that the Edmonton 1881 School — which shares a lot with it — is haunted because she's played games with its ghostly visitors.

fact. Although I haven't been to the school to see it for myself, I'm told they even have a huge poster on one of the walls at the school, documenting some of the paranormal activity that has taken place there. So, before going to the property, Rona had heard stories, but she didn't know anything specific. This was because her ghostly encounters on the grounds of the McKay School don't take place in the big main building; rather, they occurred in the little schoolhouse out back, known as the Edmonton 1881 School.

Encounters

Rona was running an evening ghost tour. They didn't have permission to go into the main building at the McKay Avenue School, which now functions as an archive and museum, but they could wander around outside and over by the small model schoolhouse in the back. It was twilight, so there was enough light for people to take photographs. Rona was giving the group instructions on how best to do that — specifically, how to maximize their chances of capturing ghosts on film.

Rona isn't sure what inspired her to do it — possibly she was led by one of her spirit guides — but she suddenly had the idea that she should ask the schoolchildren within the schoolhouse to move the window blinds. So she did. "Hey kids," she said, "if you're in there, can you move the blind poles?"

"Next thing you know," Rona told me, "they start going. Two women on the tour screamed and backed up, and one guy just started taking pictures and was like, 'This is the best tour I've ever been on, man!'"

Rona brought tours back two or three more times after that. Each time she would ask the kids to move the blind poles and each time they would comply.

The man who owned the ghost tour company Rona was working with once suggested that perhaps the movement was caused by a conveniently placed heat register, and that forced air was coming up and moving things. The problem with that, Rona's partner, Ben, pointed out, is that the little schoolhouse wasn't heated with forced air. Back in the time it was active, the room would have been heated with a little stove, not a furnace in the basement. It didn't even have a basement.

"Oh," Rona's boss said, "you mean those were real ghosts doing that?"

Suddenly, Rona said, he saw the whole thing quite differently and became quite nervous about the fact he'd been around real ghosts. So Rona couldn't resist the urge to tease him. "Yes," she said, "they are real ghosts. I hope they don't follow you home."

Connecting the Dots

Rona was recounting some of the questions she's been asked on ghost tours, specifically about this little schoolhouse. "One question, which was really a good question," Rona said, "is why would the kids be there doing that? Are they stuck there, or what's the scoop?"

Rona doesn't think they are stuck there. She didn't pick up any indication of that. In fact, she pointed out, it's possible that although they are kid-like spirits now, they didn't actually die as children.

"They could have been fully grown kids who had gone there, grew up, had a family, run a business, and died in their eighties. But they had a fun time there in that school and now when they hear somebody's there, they just appear and think, 'We're going to do some mischievous stuff for them.'

"People have to wrap their head around that. You'll see a child, but that child might be what that spirit wants to show you — the way they were. They don't want to show up as an eighty-year-old man moving blind poles."

Rona did get the feeling that the spirits in the schoolhouse were a strong, cohesive group. She thought that perhaps they had grown up together and maintained a strong lifelong connection and a spirit of fun, but there's no way that I know of to empirically make a connection between those child-like spirits and any specific people or events associated with the school.

– 19 –

Alberta Block (Former CKUA Building) — 10526 Jasper Avenue

History

Alberta Block was first built in 1909, and in the 110 years since then it has housed an incredibly diverse collection of businesses, from law firms to cigar makers. CKUA Radio was its longest-lasting tenant; it made its home there for more than fifty years, from 1955 to 2012, when it moved to its new home in the Alberta Hotel Building. The building recently underwent major renovations and refitting; today, it continues to be home to a diverse collection of businesses, including a digital arts college, a construction firm, and even a tavern.

Rona believes the sub-basement used to have an opening to a tunnel, which continued underground to the North Saskatchewan River. Back in the day, coal was brought up from mines in the river valley via the tunnel.

What We Knew Going In

I was not involved in the investigation of the CKUA building. Rona had been told that it was haunted — that was, after all, why they were investigating the site — but she didn't really know many details about the paranormal events that had been witnessed or what spirit or spirits had been seen.

Encounters

The Paranormal Explorers investigated the former CKUA building on September 23, 2005. In addition to Ben and Rona, there were two other investigators with them, Megan and Morgan. While they were there, they investigated several parts of the building, including recording studios, the 78s library, and the sub-basement. Of those areas, the most interesting and paranormally active was the sub-basement, which Rona described as being "like a highway for the spirit world."

Once down in the sub-basement, the investigators set up infrared cameras to capture any spiritual activity. From the very moment they had everything set up and switched on, orbs began to fly at them. One of the most interesting things about the orbs was that while some came straight at them, like the stars in *Star Wars* when a spaceship shifts to warp speed, others took a much slower and meandering path. If the orbs had been specks of dust moving on air currents, you would expect them to all move in the same general direction and at the same speed, but that was not the case.

Ben and Rona had to rely on the camera equipment to see the orbs, but Megan and Morgan could see them with their naked eyes. They were shocked at how large they were, and they could not contain their excitement.

In addition to seeing the orbs, they also captured a couple of really good EVPs. At one point, Rona was alone in the sub-basement, reassuring everyone over the walkie-talkie that she would be fine by herself, when a woman's voice — not Rona's, Megan's, or Morgan's — came over the walkie and said, "Hello?"

The sub-basement of the former CKUA building was like a superhighway for ghosts.

Morgan asked, "Can we see you?"

Immediately after she asked, they could hear knocking and Rona said, "What is that?" at the same time that a disembodied voice said, "Dead."

Was the ghost explaining to the investigators that they couldn't see it because it was dead? If so, is it terrible that I imagine it doing so in an exasperated tone, like we might use when explaining something we think should be obvious? Because I totally do.

Later, they were in one of the studios — Studio A. It had a piano and the walls were covered with albums. Megan took a seat on the piano bench and then jokingly said to the ghosts, "Oh, I might be sitting in your spot. I'll move, okay?"

Then they all heard someone, or something, respond: "Oh, that would be really tough on the bum," in a thick British accent.

A little later on, as part of a completely unrelated conversation, Megan happened to say the name *Charlie* and everyone in the room heard a voice say, "What did you just say?" Was it responding to hearing its name, perhaps? Or just a bit hard of hearing?

Another EVP caught Morgan and Rona chatting about a room behind the men's washroom. They heard what Rona describes as "a weird, stilted, female laugh." It wasn't any of the women on the investigation. Perhaps a female ghost had become uncomfortable with their conversation and let out a little nervous laughter?

Another odd thing happened. You know when you're talking and someone finishes your sentence for you? How irritating can that be? I know it drives me a bit batty. Imagine if it wasn't a three-dimensional person doing it, but a ghost. While the team was investigating the old CKUA building, a spirit decided to finish Rona's sentence for her. She was talking about not knowing what was on the fifth floor of the building, but a voice said the word "floor" for her before she got a chance. At least it only did it once. Imagine a ghost was always following you around finishing your sentences for you. How irksome would that be?

Speaking of potentially irritating ghosts, later on in the evening, Morgan and Rona were talking in one room about the fact that they weren't picking up anything in there. One of them suggested to the other that they might want to move and try a different room. After she said that, a spirit responded by clapping three times. "Either the spirit was happy we were leaving that room, or it was just being sarcastic."

I'd be leaning toward sarcastic myself, but I'm biased, because I just like the idea of a spirit sarcastically clapping at the ghost-hunting team being unable to spot it. Being trapped in this plane could very well make a ghost tetchy, I'd think, but perhaps I'm being overly judgmental about the ghosts.

And that, right there, is something I never would have guessed I'd ever have an occasion to say.

People, including Rona, also believe that the building is haunted by a former caretaker from the 1950s named Sam. Sam is reported to have had some intellectual disabilities — according to an *Edmonton Journal* article,[*] those disabilities were acquired when he was

---

[*] edmontonjournal.com/news/local-news/we-see-dead-people-10-spooky-edmonton-haunts-in-which-you-might-find-some-halloween-spirit

lobotomized after threatening to kill the premier of Alberta. Whatever struggles Sam had in life, Rona thinks he must have enjoyed his time in the old CKUA building and that's why he's decided to stay there after death. According to the same *Edmonton Journal* article, Sam smells strongly of cigars and is occasionally heard indulging in "operatic bellowing," a combination that, I've got to say, holds little to no appeal for me.

Connecting the Dots

None of the ghosts, with the exception of Sam, really identified themselves in any way. They seemed intent upon being seen and heard, but not necessarily recognized. And the story of Sam is pretty vague and would be difficult, if not impossible, to verify. Besides, I think the charm in Sam's story comes from thinking that someone is continuing to find joy in the place they worked, even after death, rather than in finding anything historically verifiable.

– 20 –

Scona Pool — 10450 72 Avenue NW

History

Strathcona High School, often called Scona, opened in 1908, at a time when the area of the city in which it is located was a separate city, called Strathcona. When Strathcona and Edmonton joined together, the school population outgrew the old building, and so, in 1955, it transferred to a brand-new building — the one I discuss in this chapter. A pool was added, opening shortly after, in 1956.

My research into the history of Scona High and Scona Pool did not turn up any obvious events that I can point to and say, "Oh yes! That explains everything." There are, as far as I can tell, no great tragedies or spectacular events associated with either — nothing that might serve as seeds for ghost stories. I did, however, really enjoy a little tidbit from the Scona High website (strathcona.epsb.ca/about/historyarchive/), which claims (tongue-in-cheek) that some people say there's a trap door in the crest (embedded in the floor at the main entrance) that will take you ten blocks away if you step on it.

What We Knew Going In

The entirety of this section is based on the personal experience of Tanya — a friend of a friend who is very familiar with the pool — so what Rona and I knew about the pool is completely irrelevant. Before talking to Tanya, I have to admit that I didn't know anything about the Scona Pool and hadn't heard any stories of paranormal activity associated with it. For the record, though, I hope to visit Scona Pool at some point to get a feel for the place, as well as to see first-hand the places in which Tanya's stories take place, but at time of writing I've never been there.

When I was introduced to Tanya I liked her right away. She's personable and outgoing, and she takes a very practical approach to ghosts. She believes in them, plain and simple, and why shouldn't she? She's been having paranormal encounters her whole life. "There are energies everywhere. We're never the first," she said.

I expected to sit down with Tanya and hear a couple of stories about Scona Pool, but that's not what happened. Instead, our conversation went on for more than three hours and we covered not just Scona Pool but a couple of schools and her childhood home as well.

For right now I'm going to focus on Scona Pool, but you'll hear more of Tanya's stories in later sections of this book as well.

Encounters

Tanya has been connected with the pool and the school it is attached to for many years, both directly and indirectly. Tanya has lived her whole life in that neighbourhood — on the same block, as a matter of fact. Her parents were both swim instructors at the pool. Her dad even helped to install the hydraulic basketball hoops in the school's gym, as well as the crest that is inset into the floor at the front door (which you're not supposed to step on, but people frequently do). Tanya went to school at Scona, coached there for ten years after she graduated, and also worked at the pool when she was younger. So, Tanya has a very close connection to the school and its pool.

Along with the physical connection, there's a spiritual one. It's important to note at this point that Tanya's mother was also a very spiritual woman who saw and sensed presences all through her life and just absolutely took it in stride when that happened. It seems, from what I can tell from Tanya's stories, that her mother felt as fondly toward her spirit friends as she did those she could physically touch. Talking about ghosts with Tanya, or her mother, it soon became clear that for them spirits are real, not things that might possibly exist. There are people who are physically with us, and people who have passed on but linger. And I mention this here because when Tanya started working at Scona Pool and having brushes with the paranormal, she told her mother about them and her mother's response was, "Oh, Tanya, how lovely. I'm so glad they are still there."

According to Tanya, there are several spirits at the pool — at least four, as a matter of fact. Whether Tanya's mother knew all of them is a question I don't have the answer to, but she was familiar with some of them.

Tanya and her mother aren't the only ones who have had eerie encounters at Scona Pool and school. When she worked at the pool, Tanya would frequently compare notes with her colleagues, and they told her they had often noticed the same things. More recently, when she asked one custodian if he'd experienced anything of note, he said, "I just pray to my God, miss, that he will keep me safe," and then put his earphones back in and continued on with his job. To me, that implies he has seen or heard something, even if he didn't want to share the specifics.

Most of Tanya's experiences at the pool took place between 1994 and 1997, when she was working there. A great many of the most notable encounters, Tanya recalls, took place while the school and pool were undergoing renovations to modernize the fire alarms. Rona has frequently talked about how spirits get riled up during renovations, so this did not surprise me at all.

The most prominent spirit Tanya recalls is one they called Emily. Tanya isn't sure why they named her that; it's possible it was a random name that just seemed to fit.

Tanya's description of her first encounter with Emily doesn't sound frightening at all, really. She was working in the main cashier's office and had the door open — it was after hours for the pool, so everything was locked down and she didn't need to worry about anyone wandering in. Next to the door on one side was the boys' change room, and on the other was the cashier window, which had a counter that was about four feet high. As Tanya was working, she suddenly felt as though she wasn't alone. She looked up to see a girl walk by the door to the office, her head sort of bobbing into view and back out again as she walked parallel to the cashier counter.

"I thought, well, that's weird," Tanya said, "because, like, everything is closed and why would she be coming out of a space that's the men's [change room]?"

So, curious, Tanya stood up and looked through the cashier window to see what the girl was up to. The girl did not look as though she belonged at the pool. Or in the nineties, for that matter. "I don't want to say that she looked like Laura Ingalls," Tanya said, "but she had on a white blouse, and the straps and an overdress with long hair and braids."

Rather than being disconcerted by this sight, Tanya just sort of shrugged and thought, *Oh, okay, so maybe that's Emily.* She'd already heard stories of the little girl who haunted the pool. "It's, like, a constant," Tanya explained when I asked. "You either know about it or you don't know about it. And … most of the pool employees … knew about it."

It, in this case, being Emily.

Emily was famous for calling people's names. It's unclear what she wanted when she did that — whether she did it just to get a reaction, or attention, or if there was something specific she was going for. She would also tug on the hose when people were using it.

Sometimes Emily would also hold the staff bathroom door closed. Tanya says she (and other co-workers) would use the washroom, and then when they tried to leave, the door wouldn't budge, as if it was being held from the other side. And they could hear a little girl giggling on the far side.

"And it would be like, okay, Em, very funny, but I need to go back to work now," Tanya said, and then Emily would let go of the door. She never did it when the pool was open, though, Tanya said, only early in the morning or late at night. This is interesting to me. If this is the case, then it couldn't be just some random little girl who had come to the pool and was holding the door closed, because the pool isn't open to visitors.

Emily had one favourite person she liked to interact with: a petite girl I'll call Hannah, who worked at the pool at the same time Tanya did. Whenever Hannah was working with the hose, she would feel the hose being pulled, and occasionally she would hear her name spoken from somewhere behind her. But, of course, when she looked, there was no one there. The voice always seemed to come from the direction of the change rooms, but that area is particularly echoey, so people could never pinpoint a specific location the voice was originating from.

Hannah never felt threatened by Emily and eventually got used to the tug on the hose and hearing her name spoken when there was no one around. Not everyone is quite so blasé about that sort of thing, though. There was a man who also worked at the pool, and the one time he felt the tug on the hose and heard someone call his name when no one was there, he dropped the hose and ran. He didn't want to be alone with Emily — assuming that was who had said his name — but instead surrounded himself with other people. People he could see.

Tanya got used to Miss Emily, as she called her, and actually incorporated her into her work routine. When she came in early in the mornings, she would greet the pool and then the spirits.

This routine makes total sense to me, even though I'm a skeptic, because even though Tanya didn't feel threatened by Emily or the other spirits at the pool, it's easy to see how being there alone might be unnerving. Pools are big, echoey places, and that alone is enough to be disconcerting to some; add to that the feeling (or in Tanya's case — because she has no doubts about the existence of these spirits — the knowledge) that you are not alone, and it's easy to see why some would feel decidedly nervous about being there. I can see how saying hello, breaking the silence and just putting your voice out there in a friendly gesture might be a balm on otherwise frayed nerves.

On some days, when Tanya came in to work in the mornings, she said you could feel something in the air and she'd get a little freaked out. On those days, she would actually walk outside and around to the main doors and wait for one of the regulars to show up, and then they would walk into the pool together. "I remember asking her once," Tanya recalled, "have you ever felt anything?" The regular said, "Well, some days are different from others." When Tanya talked to her about it more, asking for specifics, like whether she felt as if it was a little girl, the other woman said no. She definitely sensed a man.

She wasn't alone in feeling that way. But we'll come back to him later. Right now we're still talking about Emily.

One day, when the pool was open and Tanya was standing on deck working, she heard Emily say her name. When she looked in the direction of Emily's voice, she saw that a little boy had silently slipped into water that was too deep for him. Tanya jumped in and pulled him out. He was fine, but he might not have been — or, at the very least, might have been quite traumatized by the event — if Tanya hadn't pulled him out as quickly as she did. And Tanya might not have noticed him so fast if it hadn't been for Emily calling her name and pulling her attention in that direction.

It seems to me that Emily is a safety-conscious little girl. I really like that Emily never held the staff washroom door closed during the hours the pool was open for business. I like to think that she wouldn't want to pull a prank that kept the lifeguards away from their posts, which could have very negative consequences.

Perhaps Emily wasn't always so nice, though. On one occasion, Tanya's colleague, whom we'll call Sam, was working alone at the pool. Her task that day was to fill the pool. Filling the pool took a long time and it wasn't necessary to pay attention to things until just near the end of the operation. When the job is almost done, it becomes more important to keep an eye open. Sam was right around that crucial point where you had to pay a bit of attention. "It's one of the best parts ever," Tanya said. "You just sit and wait for the pool to fill and then you run down and turn off the valves."

Sam was hanging out on a deck chair at the side of the pool when she heard the very distinctive sound of an aluminum baton banging off the also-aluminum railing that runs from the change rooms to the deck. It was a sound she was very familiar with because the synchronized swimming coaches would bang the railing to communicate with their swimmers — the sound carries to the swimmers underwater. Sam yelled out, "We're closed, sorry." But the noise came again. And again. Not only was it continuing, but it kept getting louder and louder, and it was coming closer to her.

She couldn't see anything or anyone in the direction from which the sound was coming, and she knew logically that there couldn't be anyone there because the facility was locked up tight and she was the only one in the building.

Sam wasn't about to wait to find out who or what was swinging the baton. She left, running out the back door. The pool was still filling behind her, but she didn't care — she wasn't going to linger long enough to turn off the valves; she was out of there.

She did return eventually, once she'd had some time to gather her wits about her and steel her resolve to go in and finish her job.

Was that Emily making that noise? Tough to say. All of this sounds rather menacing, and Emily is known as more of a prankster than a scary ghost, but perhaps it was a prank that got a bigger reaction than she'd originally intended. Or maybe it was a different ghost altogether; after all, according to Tanya, there are several of them at the pool.

One of the perks of being a young adult with keys to the pool, Tanya said, was that she and her friends could gather there after hours before going out for a night on Whyte Avenue (which has a lot of clubs and bars). On one such night, several people were around and Tanya was standing on the pool deck, looking through the open door to the office. Suddenly, although she didn't feel any draft, one of the hanging plants in the office began to sway. Intrigued, Tanya watched it. The plant continued to move and then the chair in the office also moved, and not just a tiny bit: the chair slid about five or six inches across the floor before coming to a stop again.

"And I'm like, 'This is good, this is great, I'm feeling good,'" Tanya said in a tone of voice that made it clear all was not good at all. A few moments later, when her body and mind caught up to the reality of what was happening, Tanya reacted. "My system of 'freeze' doesn't work. My brain is saying, 'What are you doing? Just stand still, dummy!' and my body is like, 'Well, this can't be happening!'" And she charged forward to investigate.

There was nothing there.

I was reminded of how Rona talks about how people on investigations run toward paranormal activity instead of running away from it. I suspect Tanya would be a good companion to Rona on an investigation.

Most people, though, flee from ghosts, even ghosts like Emily. Which brings us to probably the most dramatic story about her.

As I mentioned earlier, the spirits at the pool were most active during the time when the building was undergoing renovations. Along with those renovations came people who were new to the building — workers, contractors, and inspectors — and Tanya and some of the other girls who worked at the pool at the time would tease them by saying, "If you hear your name being called, it's just Emily. You don't need to worry about it."

The workers just thought the girls were being silly and didn't take them particularly seriously. Until they did.

Because it was a school, the workers were active mostly in the late afternoon and evening. They began work when school let out and then worked into the night until the wee hours of the morning. One warm night, all the electricians working in and around the area near the pool all left within a few minutes of each other. They didn't leave because they were done their shift, or because they were tired, or even just for a cigarette break. They left because they were creeped out — and each by something different from the other. Despite the variety of things that were reported, all of the issues were blamed on Emily.

First, there were two men working in relatively close quarters to one another. Technically, they were in the school, not the pool, but they were in a part of the school that was close to the pool. They had a boom box plugged in, tuned to an FM radio station. One of the men, let's call him Ernie, was up on a ladder, and the other, whom we'll call Bert, was working down on the floor. Suddenly, the radio station changed. It didn't just go from one station to another; it switched from FM to AM, and to a station that was at totally the opposite end of the dial.

Ernie, up on his ladder and away from the radio, was like, "Dude, what are you doing? Put it back on my station." Bert didn't respond because he'd actually moved to another part of that area, so Ernie, more than a little grumpy at this point, climbed down off the ladder, changed the radio station back, barked at Bert to leave the radio alone, and climbed back up his ladder.

Just as he reached the top of his ladder, the radio station changed again. Even more annoyed, Ernie turned around to shout at Bert. Except Bert wasn't there. Ernie could see the boom box where he'd left it and, what's more, he could also see the silhouette of a young girl against the door.

That was enough for Ernie. Before you could say *Sesame Street*, he was down off the ladder and booting it away from that area and out of the building.

When Bert returned to the area where Ernie had been working, there was no sign of him, but they did run into one another outside. It turns out that around the same time Ernie saw the outline of a girl — a shadow without a subject — on the door, Bert had also looked over and seen the same thing. He'd had the same reaction as his friend and wasted no time in leaving.

I find myself wondering what it was about this outline of a girl that frightened these men so much. Was there something more to this story that they didn't tell anyone? Something that made the sight of the girl — whether coupled with the strange activity involving the radio or not — that tipped them so quickly from "Dude, leave the radio alone!" to "I'm getting the hell out of here!" without even pausing at "Well, that's weird," or something along those lines. I asked Tanya about this.

"So that's all it took?" I asked.

"That's all it took," she confirmed, and then added jokingly, "And thank you so much for coming."

During Bert and Ernie's encounter, another man was working on the school stage. Previous workers had installed pipes and this man's job was to run wires through those pipes. He was working up on a ladder, minding his own business, when, reportedly, he suddenly felt every hair on his arms and the back of his neck stand up. He didn't hesitate, he just got down off the ladder and left.

And thank you so much for coming ...

Finally, a worker who was walking near the change rooms felt confused when he heard the sound of boxes moving, and of giggling. It was about eleven o'clock at night, so there should not have been anyone in those change rooms at all. The worker decided to use the master key that had been lent to him to open the door and chase the kids out of there.

As he slid the key into the lock, he distinctly heard the sound of a kid whisper, "Shhh, somebody's coming!"

Then he opened the door.

The room was empty of people, but he could still hear the sound of boxes being moved around.

And thank you so much for coming ...

All four electricians abandoned the building within the span of about five minutes, each for related but different eerie experiences.

"The supervisors came out to talk to [Sam] and me, and they were like, 'What is going on here?' Because the workers had all left and said that we knew what was going on," Tanya recalled. "And we just looked at each other like, *We are never going to have a job again, but okay, here we go ...*"

The supervisors weren't particularly open to the idea that their workers had been driven away by paranormal happenings, but the workers seemed to be. Tanya said she even heard that the man on the stage went so far as to write a letter to the entity he'd encountered.

In the letter, the electrician wrote, "You know, I don't know what you're about or who you are, but I'm just here to do my job.... I don't want you to leave, I just need you to let me do my job to keep the kids safe."

I'm exceptionally curious about this, because where does one send a letter to a ghost? I imagine that the catharsis or magic of it comes in the writing — assuming you write it in a space where the ghost can see you doing it — but still ... then what? Do you keep it? Burn it? Just leave it on the stage? These are the sorts of details that the fiction writer in me really wants to cling to and chew on ... even though they probably aren't relevant to this story.

Emily isn't the only spirit Tanya says is lingering at the pool. There is a ghost who is generally referred to as "the Indian." I know ... it makes me uncomfortable even writing that, but it's what they call him. I don't know what to tell you.

Anyway ...

One afternoon, the pool was rented out for a birthday party. One of the children attending the party was a regular at the pool, so Tanya knew him fairly well. For this story, we'll call him Daniel. Daniel was about eight years old at this time, and during the party he came out of the washroom and was walking along the deck. There's nothing unusual about that, of course, but once he came alongside the basketball hoop, he just started laughing.

"It wasn't a fake laugh," Tanya told me. "It was a belly laugh."

"Daniel," she said. "What are you laughing at there, buddy?"

"The Indian," he said.

Tanya looked. There was no one there. Daniel, as far as she could tell, was laughing at empty space. "An Indian," she said, dubious but wanting to confirm what he'd said.

"He's so funny," Daniel said. "Why can't you see him? He's so funny."

Tanya said, "Well, is he nice?"

Through his laughter, Daniel said that, yes, he was nice, and again wondered why Tanya couldn't see him.

Tanya said she wasn't sure why she couldn't see him, but decided that if Daniel said he was nice, then he could stay; she wouldn't ask him to leave. Daniel eventually continued off on his way, but about five minutes later, he came back to the same spot and started giggling again.

"Is he still in my pool?" Tanya asked. Daniel confirmed that he was and again said how funny he was. Tanya again said he could stay.

After work, Tanya went home and told her mom about the incident. She didn't tell her in a sincere way, more in a "Mom, you will not believe what this ridiculous kid was doing at the pool today" way. Her mother's response surprised her.

"Oh, Tanya," her mother said. "How nice. He was there when I used to work there. I'm so glad he's still there."

When her mother worked at the pool, she'd see him wearing full buckskin clothing and long braids, standing at the edge of the pool. Each time they encountered one another, he would nod to her, and she, being polite, would nod back. And that's just how it was. Tanya's mother never found him nearly as hilarious as Daniel did, but she didn't think he was dangerous, either.

Scary Guy, on the other hand … well, as you might guess from his name, he wasn't anyone's favourite spirit.

When you enter the pool through the common entrance it shares with the school, there are some doors and a few stairs, and then there is a long hallway. Often, people walking down that hallway would feel a presence. A sort of heaviness. Tanya compared it to smoke, something that made it difficult to breathe. As in a room full of smoke, people felt that, to breathe clearly, they needed to get lower to the ground, to where the fresh air is. This spirit was sort of like that. He inhabited the space and made the air heavy. "You would almost want to crouch," Tanya said. Except, of course, that might slow you down, and no one wanted to linger in that hallway.

"It wasn't sad," she said. "And it wasn't angry. It was just … you were not alone and it wasn't pleased."

Tanya wasn't the only one who felt it. One of the regular morning swimmers also said she felt it on occasion.

The description of the feeling being like smoke that fills a space and presses you down reminds me a bit of "Big Black," a giant shadow person so big it fills the hallway, which is said to haunt Waverly Hills Sanatorium. I wrote about Big Black in *Haunted Hospitals* and the hospital he's said to haunt is in Kentucky, not Edmonton, so I won't go into detail about it here, but it does make me wonder if the two phenomena — Big Black and Scary Guy — could be related somehow.

Scary Guy isn't just responsible for the dark, unwelcoming feeling in the hallway, though; he also lifts weights.

There is a weight room in that area, and sometimes at night when the pool employees are doing their final big clean before locking up and going home, they see the twenty-five-pound weights moving around. Not, like, levitating through the air, but definitely moving. They would be put away on the weight rack, but they would be moving back and forth and clanking together.

Tanya, making it clear there was no mechanical explanation she could think of, pointed out that it's a solid concrete building, so very structurally sound. "Yes," she admitted, "we're close to train tracks, but nothing else in the room was moving, just the weights."

Interesting side note: Emily doesn't want anything do with Scary Guy, either. Tanya said that as far as she knows, no one has ever had an encounter with Emily in the same space that Scary Guy usually inhabits. I can't say I blame her. A ghost who can shift around twenty-five-pound weights and has a bad attitude is not one I would want to deal with. No wonder they call him Scary Guy!

The third ghost Tanya says inhabits the pool is one they call Hank. Hank largely hangs around the chemical areas and the filtration room. Tanya told me you can smell Hank. "Emily is the only ghost who will call names or giggle, but Hank is the only one who has an odour."

And it's not a pleasant odour. Tanya said it's something akin to greasy, unwashed hair and it's very distinctive. I've got to think, given that they smell him in the chemical areas of a pool, which must have a strong smell already of chlorine and whatnot, the odour must be very powerful.

But Tanya and some of her former co-workers haven't just smelled Hank; they've also seen him. Well, parts of him. They will occasionally catch a glimpse of his upper body out of the corner of their eye. Hank wears a white-and-blue-striped shirt with long sleeves, buttons, and a collar. Tanya's impression was of an old CN Rail shirt.

Tanya and a co-worker believe they saw Hank in his entirety one day … and they didn't even realize it until after the fact. On that day, the city employee who was tasked with maintaining the pool's boilers came. Tanya and her colleague approached him and asked if there was something wrong, because they had both just seen him — or thought they had — downstairs. "Nothing is wrong," he assured them. He was just there to test things out. When they asked why he had to come back so quickly — after all, they'd just seen him a few minutes ago — he shook his head. "I wasn't here a few minutes ago," he said.

When they looked closer, they realized the maintenance man and the man they'd seen in the basement were wearing different shirts. They had both seen Hank downstairs and he looked so normal and human they hadn't even realized he was a spirit until afterward.

Hank is never menacing or heavy like Scary Guy. He is just sort of occasionally there and people will smell him or catch a glimpse of his distinctive shirt. And since he hangs out exclusively in the chemical storage room and the filtration room, he is pretty much out of the way and not really a bother to anyone.

Tanya learned about the fourth ghost that haunts the pool and school area when she was talking to her mother, who asked Tanya about the lady upstairs.

"What lady upstairs?" Tanya asked a bit warily.

At the time Tanya's mother worked at the pool, she had a key that would give her access to parts of the school — greater access than Tanya had when she worked there. Her mother, while locking up, would occasionally hear the sound of someone in high heels walking across the gymnasium floor. Fully expecting to encounter a ghost, her mother would go up into the gym to talk with her. She would definitely hear the heels click-clacking across the gym floor, but she never actually saw anyone there, ghostly or otherwise, with whom to have a conversation.

Intrigued by this new information, Tanya began asking around to see if anyone else had heard the lady in high heels; it turns out, several people had. They would feel a woman walking about two or three paces behind them, and they'd hear her high heels. But if they turned around, no one was there.

Connecting the Dots

There's just no way for me to connect the ghosts Tanya has encountered at the pool with any specific incident or individual. As the building is near railway tracks, it's possible that Hank is just a former CN Rail employee whose affinity for boilers and steam continued into his afterlife. Perhaps Emily is the spirit of a pioneer who died on those grounds long before there was a school, or a pool, or even a city of Edmonton. I'm a storyteller; I could certainly make up some compelling stories ... but the truth is there aren't any obvious dots to connect. Happily, that doesn't diminish the power of the stories Tanya shared one bit.

Queen Elizabeth School — 9425 132 Avenue NW

History

Queen Elizabeth School's (or Queen E, as it is often fondly call) history must be pretty mundane, because I haven't been able to find out much about it at all. According to Wikipedia, the school was founded in 1960 … I can't believe I just cited Wikipedia as a source for information on this school, but its official website doesn't have any information about its history at all, and desperate times call for desperate measures.

What We Knew Going In

Exactly like the preceding chapter, this section relies solely on a single source, that being Tanya; therefore, what Rona and I knew ahead of time is irrelevant. According to Tanya, there are spirits everywhere, so while she wasn't entering the school with the intention of locating spirits, she would not have been surprised to encounter them.

Encounters

Tanya teaches at Queen E. As we all know, a teacher's job doesn't end when the school bell rings, so she frequently comes in on the weekends to get more done.

"I will walk in, and I'll say 'Hello, school,' and the radio in the basement [will come] on," Tanya said.

Once she asked the custodian about the phenomenon, looking for what Tanya called a "mechanical explanation."

"Do you leave that radio on all the time?" she asked.

"Yes," was his blunt response, offered in a way that did not want to encourage further discussion. Tanya was not so easily dissuaded, though. The radio wasn't on when she'd first arrived, but had turned on after she said hello.

"Is it alarmed so it goes on and off by itself [under certain circumstances]?"

"No," he said.

"So ..." she said, "it just comes on by itself sometimes?"

And he said, "Yup."

End of conversation, right? But no, not really. Tanya said they exchanged a meaningful look and then he continued, "There's always stuff going on behind me when I'm working. I can see things out of the corner of my eye, but whoever is there, we have an understanding. I'm here to do a job; they are here to continue whatever job it was they never finished."

That made total sense to Tanya, but she did note that the school has so many cameras now it would be interesting to monitor them and see if anything came up. Not even necessarily to catch evidence of spirit activity — although that would be cool — but just to watch her reaction to the school. "Because oftentimes," she said, "I'll come in and I'll hear something and just stop in my tracks with my coffee in my hand and my key chain swinging back and forth [from a lanyard]. And I'm just standing there, staring. Waiting for something to come out of the Math hallway." (Spoiler: nothing ever does.)

"You're like one of those cats that freak me out when they just stare at nothing," I said.

"Yeah," Tanya agreed, but then added, "but there's something there. There's something there."

One time, when Tanya was walking by the classroom that used to belong to the Math Department head, she heard a sound, as though there was a great wind blowing inside the room. It sounded as if there was a huge windstorm outside and someone had left the windows to that classroom open. Tanya could hear the vertical blinds flapping as well as the sound of papers being blown violently about.

Tanya knew the logical thing to do was call security — there was no telling what was on the other side of that door; it could be an intruder, for all she knew. It wasn't unheard of. In the past, if someone accidentally forgot to secure a window, people had broken in and stolen electronics by taking them back out the window. So, she knew she should go back out into the parking lot and wait for security and their dogs to arrive, but she didn't. Instead, she approached the door, key in hand.

"I am an Edmonton public school employee," she shouted at the door. "I'm coming to the door...."

The whole time she was walking up to the door and putting her key in the lock, she was shouting a play-by-play to the classroom, hoping that if someone was in there they would leave or, at the very least, not be startled into doing something foolish. And while she was delivering this running commentary — "I'm coming closer to the door. I'm putting my key in the door ..." — she could still hear the ferocious wind in the room, and the sound of papers being tossed about.

But as soon as she opened the door, the sound stopped.

There was nothing.

No windows were open. Nothing was out of place in the classroom. It was just an everyday, empty classroom. The only sound was the tick, tick, tick of the second hand moving on the clock.

But when she went back into the hallway, she heard the same sound coming from another classroom. When she opened that door, again, it was the exact same thing.

When Tanya or the custodian arrive at the school and see the other person's car in the parking lot, they will whistle or call "yoo-hoo" once they arrive in the building. When they hear that cue, the person already in the building will respond back in kind. It's a shorthand way to let the other person know they are no longer alone in the building and, further, tells them exactly who else is there with them. One time, Tanya was in the washroom, and she heard someone whistle and do the yoo-hoo, so she called back "yoo-hoo," but there was no response.

When she was finished in the washroom, she went out into the hallway, and there was no one there. So she checked the parking lot, but hers was the only car there. That left her feeling rather uncomfortable.

As does the Drama hallway.

"I refuse to go down the Drama hallway when I'm alone in the school," Tanya said, "even when all the lights are on." She didn't specify why, which is interesting because Tanya is one of those people who runs toward the paranormal activity, not away from it, but that hallway is a no-go zone for her, except during normal school hours or times when she knows she's not alone in the building.

There are several places in the school Tanya won't go without the lights on. She said that her students have noticed and asked her about it. She said she tells them that's because at the end of the lights is where they'll find her body. "Just follow the lit path," she jokes. She'll be in the darkness at the end of it.

When she says that, she is joking, but it's the kind of joke with real emotion behind it. Real … if not fear, at least discomfort.

Connecting the Dots

Although I couldn't find out any history of the building and although neither Rona nor I have ever visited the school, it's okay. In the end, the eerie experiences Tanya shared with me that were associated with Queen E would be impossible to pin to a specific person or even event associated with the school. So if there is no detailed history to provide, it's all right because there are no dots to connect, anyway. Not really.

- 22 -

Masonic Order Freemasons Hall of Edmonton — 10318 100 Avenue NW

History

According to the Alberta Freemasons website at freemasons.ab.ca, "Freemasonry is one of the world's oldest secular fraternal societies." It's the sort of secretive society that tends to inspire whispered stories, conspiracy theories, and all sorts of other imaginative ideas, but according to architect and Mason Darrel Babuk, speaking in a CBC interview, "The Masons are not a secret society; [they are, rather] a society with secrets."* Either way, they also happen to be a group that, being founded by masons, know a thing or two about creating a beautiful building.

The Freemasons Hall on 100 Avenue is definitely a beautiful building. It's a four-storey structure, built in the Gothic tradition, and it's absolutely beautiful, inside and out. Completed in 1931 and opened

---

* cbc.ca/news/canada/edmonton/capital-foundations-freemasons-edmonton-1.4784690

in 1932, it is, according to that same CBC interview, one of the few surviving Masonic lodges in the city. It contains what's left of the city's first library and also the oldest passenger elevator in the province. Available now for those wishing to rent it for social functions, it also still hosts secret Mason meetings.

What We Knew Going In

Neither Rona nor I actually visited this location for the purposes of a paranormal investigation. I did visit the building once, when some friends of mine rented it for their wedding. At the time I had no idea about any eerie stories surrounding it, and just thought it was a lovely building and a great location for a wedding. This section will be drawn solely from the experiences of a friend of mine, Chadwick. He is not from Edmonton, and so was completely unfamiliar with the location and its history before his visit.

Encounters

Chadwick Ginther, an award-winning author of darkly delightful works of fiction from Winnipeg, Manitoba, was in Edmonton some years ago on a book tour. It was the last day of the tour and Chadwick had a little extra time on his hands, so one of his local friends, who just happened to be a Mason, offered to take him for lunch and then show him the lodge. Chadwick accepted and enjoyed a tour of the building.

Toward the end of the visit, the tour guide mentioned the ghost face in the window. He said it casually, like it was just an accepted fact that *of course* there was a ghost face in the window, and why wouldn't there be?

Chadwick was, of course, intrigued, so they all went outside to the parking lot behind the lodge and, sure enough, there was a ghost face in the window.

Now, the ghostly face that is visible in the window seems like the sort of thing that might be easily explained away. It could be a curtain or an object inside the room, or the image could just be caused by

A ghostly face looks out a window in the Masonic Hall. It's not only the face that is mysterious, though. No one has been able to find this window from inside the building.

weird light on the window glass, right? Right. But the thing about this ghostly face in the window is, Chadwick's tour guide insisted, no one has been able to find that specific window inside the building. And apparently people have even taken hammers to the walls to look for it.

So, for me, the eerie part about this story isn't necessarily the face in the window — although that is intriguing — but the window itself, which can be located only from outside the building.

Connecting the Dots

Honestly, I don't know if the Masons are a secret society or a society with secrets, but I can't think of a more appropriate building in the city to have a mysterious window that no one can locate from the outside. It's just perfect.

– 23 –

Strathcona Museum, Sherwood Park — 913 Ash Street, Sherwood Park

History

The building that now houses the Strathcona Museum was originally built in 1959 and used as the very first fire hall for Sherwood Park. Then, in 1967, it was adapted to house the city's first Royal Canadian Mounted Police (RCMP) station as well. By 1992, however, both the fire department and the RCMP had relocated to different buildings, so a few years later, in March of 1995, the county agreed to let the Strathcona County Heritage Foundation use the empty building as a museum.

The museum officially opened on July 12, 1997. Currently, it has permanent exhibits dedicated to the RCMP and firefighting, and models of a one-room school, a train station, a grain elevator, and more.

What We Knew Going In

I have never visited Strathcona Museum before I began working on this book. Rona, however, knew before her very first visit to the museum that ghosts had been spotted there. She knew because she'd been called to visit it in an official capacity after someone working there had a very harrowing experience. Rona's partner, Ben, is the one who actually took that call. He got all the information about what had happened, but he kept that from Rona because he wanted to see if her experience would compare with that of the other woman if she didn't know any details beforehand.

Encounters

Funny story: as Ben and Rona, along with a couple of other paranormal investigators, were driving to the museum to investigate the occurrence there, they drove up behind an SUV with a vanity licence plate that read HAUNTED. Now if that doesn't set the atmosphere for a paranormal investigation, I don't know what would.

Right after arriving to investigate, Rona headed down into the basement. As she entered a very dark back room, which was lit only by the meagre light from her camera, she had a very negative feeling, as though something was threatening her, and an impression of something coming up behind her and stabbing her in the back. When she turned around to see if someone was there, a man lunged out of the wall toward her with his arms outstretched like he was going to strangle her. The spirit gave off a very malevolent, violent vibe, and he transferred the thought to Rona that he dealt with everything in a very physical way.

Startled by the sudden appearance of a ghost and his aggressive movement, Rona took a couple of steps backward, never taking her eyes off the spirit. "Ben," she called up the stairs, "I need you to come down here and bring the video camera." Unfortunately, by the time Ben made it down the stairs, the spirit had disappeared, but not before Rona had gotten some really strong impressions from him.

"What I got from him," Rona told me as we sat in my dining room with my cats climbing all over us, "was that he had been a prisoner. I don't know how he died, but he thought it was pretty fun that he could hang out in the [former] RCMP quarters, where they used to sleep at night … and [he] enjoyed slowly walking up the hallway to scare whoever was working late."

When Rona told the museum's manager and curator what she'd seen in the basement, the woman told her that same menacing spirit had stalked her down a hallway and, in fact, that was why she'd asked Ben and Rona to come investigate.

She also relayed a story about a student who was working as an intern at the museum. According to the story, the student had set up a little working space in what had once been a jail cell and was cataloguing artifacts in there when suddenly the incredibly heavy metal door slammed shut behind her. The door was far too heavy (275 kilograms) to have been closed by an errant breeze or by itself. Indeed, it took several people to reopen it. Did a ghost slam it shut? It's definitely a possibility. Perhaps it was the same one who likes to scare people in the basement.

After encountering the violent spirit in the basement, Rona went to the schoolroom display — a permanent exhibit that shows a 1920s-era schoolroom and includes desks, science displays, and the Clover Bar School bell — and sat in one of the desks. From there, Rona saw tiny pinpoints of light that seemed to dance around the room, which told Rona she was in the company of spirits. While she sat and watched the sparkles of light, she picked up the names of two kids: Leah, and the nickname Smiley. None of the spirits were able to fully materialize, however, so Rona was unable to get more detailed information about them.

In the main part of the museum, the walls don't quite meet the ceiling and the space between where the walls end and the ceilings begin is used for storage. Later, while she was upstairs, Rona could feel several spirits up in that storage space, watching them as they continued to investigate the museum, but she wasn't able to really zero in on them and pick up very many details about them. She did manage to pick up four names, though — Wilson, McNamara, Scrubber (which one hopes is a nickname), and Tessa.

According to an October 30, 2015, article in the *Edmonton Journal* by Brent Wittmeier, Starr Hanson — the museum's manager and curator — says an RCMP guard and a prisoner have been known to frequent the museum, but she claims both of them are friendly. Further, strong odours like licorice, matchsticks, and pipe smoke have also been reported. Starr doesn't mind sharing her workspace with the spirits. "People ask if I'd like a ceremony to have them removed," the *Edmonton Journal* quoted her as saying. "I say they're not hurting anything, so I'm not afraid to have them here."

Connecting the Dots

It is interesting that Rona came to the museum not knowing what the person who called her had experienced, and then encountered what could be exactly the same dark entity. And it's not an especially difficult mental stretch to think that a man of that character — who solves problems through violence and enjoys scaring people — would have been familiar with the building when it was still a functional jail. Further, it seems to me like that sort of person really would get a kick out of sleeping where his former captors slept, and perhaps by locking innocent interns in jail cells. The pieces of the story all fit.

As for the spirits upstairs, well … that whole floor is filled with displays of old items, many of which probably belonged to people who have since died. If one believes that spirits can become attached to belongings (and the proliferation of possessed dolls, cursed jewellery and haunted paintings I see in books and movies tells me that many people do believe that), it's easy to imagine quite a wide range of spirits who have made the upstairs gallery their home. Or at least who visit from time to time.

Funny story, though. I was talking to Geri Dittrich at the Walterdale Theatre about the urban legend that says the bell at their theatre (which, you will recall, used to be a fire hall) has been heard ringing when no one is around. Geri told me she'd never heard anyone from the theatre talk about that, nor had she experienced it herself. "But," she asked, "have you ever heard about the bell at the Strathcona Museum ringing late at night? Because if so, that might have been me."

I had not heard of any mysterious bell-ringing at the Strathcona Museum, but still, I was intrigued and asked her to tell me the story.

"Several years ago, when the museum was just starting to get put together, I was working with another theatre company and I needed a room. So they [the people in charge of the Strathcona Museum] allowed me to put the company's costumes in the basement ... and they gave me a room to work in. So I had a workshop in there," she said. "I also had a key to the back door."

Geri became friendly with the staff and volunteers at the museum, and they would frequently come by her room in the basement to have a coffee and chat, or whatnot. And whenever someone new came to the museum — a new hire, volunteer, or exhibitor — they would get a tour of the museum that included a stop in Geri's workshop, and introductions.

One day Geri was introduced to a man who had a collection he was hoping to exhibit at the museum. I'm going to be vague about what his display featured, for reasons that ought to become clear soon enough. Let's pretend it was pianos. It was not pianos, but they will work just fine as a stand-in for this story.

He and a staff member were walking around the facility, checking the doors to see if they were large enough to accommodate his collection, when they encountered Geri and introductions were made. Then the man and the staff member carried on to the next door.

That night, around midnight, Geri got a sudden chill, like someone had left a door open, so she started to go through the building to check.

None of the doors open from the outside but, Geri thought, someone looking to see if a door would be big enough to get a "piano" in could easily slip something in the latch so that it didn't lock properly, if that someone had a reason to want to be able to covertly access the building later.

Her creepy feeling intensified. Rather than check all the doors in a dark building in which she couldn't be sure she was alone, Geri took another, quite unexpected course of action.

"They had an old school bell in there," Geri said. "And I took it, and I rang it until I was almost deaf. I rang it and I rang it and I rang it. I went back to my room, got my coat and my purse and I went out the door."

A few days later, she was talking to a friend who lived several blocks away from the museum. The bemused friend confessed to Geri, "I heard bells. It was the damnedest thing. Nobody could explain it."

Geri and I had a good laugh at the thought that her unorthodox method of dealing with what might have been an intruder could actually have become the basis for a new urban legend. Which, of course, made the skeptical part of me wonder how many other ghost stories have unusual but very terrestrial explanations.

However, one still has to wonder if the reason Geri was creeped out in the first place was because she was sensing the dark spirit that had menaced Rona and slammed the jail cell door on the intern. After all, Geri *was* working in the basement....

PART TWO:
PRIVATE RESIDENCES

– 24 –

Private Residences:
A Different Approach

The other sections of this book, those dealing with public buildings and businesses, were subdivided into segments — "History," "What We Knew Going In," "Encounters," "Connecting the Dots." The address of each location was provided. However, as we move into this part of the book, dealing with private residences, I'm going to change things up some.

First of all, I won't be revealing the addresses of the homes where these encounters occurred. Second, I won't be dividing these sections into segments. That is because neither Rona nor I have ever visited any of these residences — as far as we can remember, anyway.

I will simply be retelling stories that were told to me. As I did with all the stories in the previous sections, I will be relaying everything I am told because, again, it is not my job to question whether what people tell me is accurate or not. My job is to share the stories in such a way that you, the reader, can do it for yourself.

I won't be discussing the history of these locations, except to relay what has been told to me by the people who shared their stories.

There are two reasons for this: first, as the residences are private, most of them will have pretty boring histories; and second, as I said, I don't want to reveal the addresses, just the neighbourhood.

I think it's important that I not share the addresses of these homes. Although many of the people who told me their ghost stories no longer live in the houses where the hauntings occurred, some still do. Either way, whoever lives in those houses has the right to not have to worry about ghost hunters or paranormal investigators knocking on their doors.

– 25 –

Brittney — Knottwood Area (Millwoods)

When I asked on Twitter if anyone in Edmonton had a ghost story to share, Brittney Le Blanc was one of the first, and most enthusiastic, people to contact me. "My childhood home was haunted," she said. It wasn't a scary place to grow up, though, according to Brittney, and her family never felt threatened by the strange goings-on in their home.

Brittney's bedroom was in the basement and the door would frequently open and shut all by itself. It didn't seem to matter if it was fully latched; it would still just open and close, over and over again — even if she and her family were in the nearby downstairs family room. They didn't feel menaced by the door's movements; the family thought they were odd but pretty much just accepted it as a thing that just sometimes happened. This is something I've noticed a lot in speaking with people about their paranormal experiences — if the unexplained events aren't accompanied by any feeling of danger or threat, people seem to quickly accept them as part of their new normal. It's interesting, the sorts of things we can get used to.

Brittney's family didn't just have a door that opened and closed by itself to become used to; they also had to deal with an artwork that inexplicably fell down all the time. The piece had been created by a dying man for his son. The son didn't want it and it ended up at Brittney's family's home. The framed work, which depicted a ship, had been created using big, chunky pieces of wood mounted on a heavy canvas background — so it was not dainty or light. And it had a mind of its own. No matter how or where they hung the artwork, in very short order they would discover it on the floor, leaning up against the wall. Given the way the artwork was leaning, it was obvious that it hadn't simply fallen from the wall and ended up there; it felt very much more like it had been carefully taken off the wall and leaned up against it, instead. Except no one had done that. No one with a physical body, anyway …

There were other odd happenings in the house, too. Once, Brittney and her family were watching *Ginger Snaps* in the basement living room, which, as Brittney noted, is about as Edmonton-y as you can get. There was a bag of empty pop cans tucked into a corner of the room and all of a sudden the cans started falling out of the bag. One might think, *Well, gravity, right?* Except, in this case the cans had to *rise up* before they could tumble of the bag, which is impossible according to the law of gravity.

And that wasn't even the most dramatic ghost moment the family had in that house.

When Brittney was a teenager, the family decided to paint the upstairs living room. As a group, they'd moved all the furniture to the middle of the floor, covered everything up, taped the walls, primed them, and painted the first coat. Then, deciding to take a break in some fresh air that didn't reek of paint, they all went out for lunch at a restaurant, leaving all their painting supplies — rollers, trays, paint, brushes, tape — on a paint sheet in the middle of the floor. They locked the door behind them when they left and assumed the house was secure. When they came home, the door was still locked, but all of their paint and painting supplies were missing. "No paint supplies," Brittney told me. "No rollers. No paint trays. It was all missing!"

They searched the house from top to bottom but could not find any of the vanished supplies anywhere. Eventually, they actually ended up repurchasing all the supplies. They also needed to colour-match the paint on the walls to be sure the new paint they bought would match. What an ordeal!

Some years later, they moved away from that house. They completely emptied it and packed up, but the paint supplies never resurfaced.

Brittney wonders if the spirit, or spirits, in her childhood home might be related to some of the objects in the home, like that ship piece, which had once belonged to people who had passed. "My mom always liked to bring home objects from the recently deceased," she said. That included not only the ship artwork; she even brought a hospital bed, in which any number of deaths might have occurred.

"Moral of the story? Stop bringing home dead people's things," Brittney concluded.

– 26 –

Chloe — Central Edmonton

Chloe's story takes place in a house, but not her house. From late January to early February, she and her husband were keeping their realtor busy showing them houses in central Edmonton. They visited more than twenty houses in those weeks, trying to find the one that was perfect for them.

At one point, the realtor took them to a house Chloe described as "rundown, but still a cute little 1950s bungalow." The three of them — Chloe, her husband, and the realtor — entered the house to discover that none of the lights worked. It gets dark super early in Edmonton in January and February, so this wasn't just a minor inconvenience; it was dark outside and even darker inside because it didn't benefit from any streetlights. The realtor left Chloe and her husband at the door and ventured inside, where he discovered that the lights in the back half of the house worked. They still had to brave the pitch-black living room to make it to the lit areas. Not exactly an uncreepy way to begin a tour of an empty house; still, they felt comfortable enough at that point that the three of them split up to check out the house.

Chloe walked into a bedroom. There wasn't anything unusual about it; it was just an empty bedroom. Or was it? When she turned to look behind her, the door slowly closed. No one had moved it; there was no draft that would explain it: it just crept closed while she watched.

It didn't stay closed long because the realtor, whom Chloe described as being "unflappable" in most situations, suddenly came in, his face pale, and asked her if she'd done that. She obviously hadn't; she was standing in the middle of the room and hadn't moved at all.

Chloe wondered if perhaps the house was just crooked and gravity was working its magic, closing the door even though no one had touched it. Before Chloe and the realtor had a chance to convince themselves that was what had happened, they heard Chloe's husband yell from the basement and then come stomping up the stairs. They could clearly see a goose egg developing on his head.

While he'd been in the basement, he said, he'd felt a presence, as if he wasn't alone and whatever was there with him objected to them being in the house. And then something had smashed him in the side of the head with a door. "It felt like it had been pushed into me," he said.

The three of them decided they wanted nothing more to do with that house and left as quickly as they could.

"It was the most unsettling building I've ever been in," Chloe said.

– 27 –

Janice — Kilkenny

Janice used to study at her friend's house across the street from M.E. LaZerte High School. It was a nondescript bungalow that had been built in the late sixties. Nothing about it stuck out as being spooky or haunted, but then her friend asked, "You want to see something weird?" and called Janice into his mother's bedroom. He opened the closet doors and invited her to stick her hand in.

"Being that ridiculously brave that comes with knowing nothing and everything, I stretched out my hand toward the clothes hanging in front of me," she told me. As soon as she reached into the closet, all the hairs on her arm stood up and her arm got all goosebumpy. She was reaching through extremely cold air. By waving her hand around, she was able to determine that it was a column of cold air about six feet tall and roughly the size of a person.

"I also met an angel," she said, nonchalantly, as if that's something that happens to everyone, every day.

The angelic encounter didn't take place at the friend's house, but rather at the University of Alberta Hospital. Janice was as scared as she'd ever been that day. She was a young single mother and she'd just had day surgery to remove a suspicious lump in her breast. As she exited the unit, she went into the open atrium area part of the hospital — a part in which, night or day, people are usually around. During the day, there are generally enough people that you can hear a low-key people buzz interspersed with occasional louder exclamations: someone dropping a tray in the cafeteria, a child squealing in delight or anger, that sort of thing. But there was none of that. It was empty, quiet. Creepy.

Janice hurried over to the elevator, and as she waited, a really big Indigenous man, about ten years older than her, approached and stood beside her, also facing the elevator, as though waiting.

"I'm not hitting on you, and don't want you to feel uncomfortable, but you are very beautiful and your life is good," he said.

Janice says she smiled. In spite of her fears of cancer and stranger danger, she smiled. Before she had a chance to respond further, though, the elevator arrived and the door opened. She stepped in and turned to face the open door, as we all do in elevators, and the man wasn't there. Nor was he anywhere in sight, and because the elevators in the atrium at the University Hospital are glass, Janice had a very good view of the place.

"I had to wait a week to find out the lymph node was benign," Janice concluded. "And my life was good."

− 28 −

Corinne — Glenora

When I first met Corinne, it was in a context that had absolutely nothing to do with ghosts, but as soon as she learned I was collecting ghost stories for this book, she said, "Oh, have I got a story for you." And she was not wrong.

Corinne was living with some friends in a house in Glenora. This particular house was more than a hundred years old; it had four storeys above ground and a roughed-out basement that was home to an ancient boiler. She described it as "both beautiful and vaguely creepy." Her friends had rented the house while Corinne was living out of the country, and when she returned to Edmonton, she moved in with them. When Corinne moved in, her friends told her that in addition to the living occupants (she, her friends, and their Weimaraner), she would be sharing the space with a ghost they'd named Errol.

(As a total side note, I have heard a lot of ghost names while working on this book and *Haunted Hospitals,* and Errol is absolutely my favourite. Hands down.)

Anyway, apparently Errol had a flair for the dramatic. Corinne's friends claimed that one time, before she moved in, he had ripped their big showcase mirror off the wall and thrown it against the wall opposite, smashing it.

Clearly, the ghost wanted attention. He quite often got it from the dog. Sometimes the dog would stop whatever she was doing and stare, alert and aware, at something in the middle distance that Corinne couldn't see.

Speaking of the dog, she was pretty clever and had been trained to ring a bell that was tied to the back door whenever she wanted to go outside. One night, it was just Corinne and the dog alone in the big, creaky house. They were hanging out in the TV room on the fourth floor when the dog meandered away. Shortly after, Corinne heard the bell ring on the back door two floors below. So, Corinne went downstairs to let the dog out.

While the dog was out doing her thing, Corinne double-checked that all the windows and the front door were securely locked. She said she did this "partly out of routine and partly because it was slightly unsettling to be the only person in that house. It wasn't scary — it was just ... slightly eerie in the way that old houses are." Everything was closed up tight, and once Corinne had let the dog in and locked up behind her, they went back upstairs to finish the movie.

About a quarter of an hour later, Corinne heard the bell ring. She'd been so immersed in the movie that she hadn't felt the dog move off the couch. She stood up somewhat reluctantly to let the dog out again. It wasn't until Corinne reached the TV room's door that she realized the dog was still on the sofa. In fact, the dog looked quite confused about where Corinne was going. As Corinne was standing there, trying to figure out if she'd imagined the bell ringing, it rang again. Sharply. Distinctly.

Corinne called the dog to her and they went back downstairs together.

Corinne said she thought, "Oh, I've forgotten to secure it and the wind is catching it," but I can't help but wonder if she was only trying to convince herself that was the case, because would you really need the moral support of the dog if you thought you were going downstairs to face a breeze? Perhaps. Being all alone in a big, old house is enough to put anyone on edge, so maybe that was the sole reason she called the dog to her, but maybe part of her knew that this story wasn't over yet.

Once they got downstairs, she discovered that everything was still secure. There was no wind — not even a draft. All the doors and windows were locked up tight, just as they had been when she and the dog went upstairs fifteen minutes before.

Reassured, they went back upstairs to finish their movie. Only a few minutes later, she heard the bell ring again. So did the dog. Her ears perked up and she watched Corinne as the bell rang sharply several times before falling silent. "We," Corinne said, "decided mutually not to check it out that time, and I turned up the TV."

Once the movie was finished, Corinne took the bell off the door for the night — eliminating any chance of it disturbing her sleep — and invited the dog into her room.

Later, once her friends had returned from their trip, they all tried to reproduce the incident, jostling the bell in several different ways, but they were never able to re-create the effect. Eventually, of course, the blame was placed squarely upon Errol.

- 29 -

Daryl — McKernan

Daryl's house in McKernan sits on land that was once a lake. McKernan Lake was drained and filled in the 1940s, and much of the neighbourhood is built on the old lake bed.

Daryl lived with his wife, Jill, and his daughter, Alexa, in a house they had purchased from friends. Their friends, Allen and Sharon (not their real names), had loved the house and renovated it extensively, including building a new bedroom for their daughter, but in 2004, Allen accepted a new job in Michigan and sold the home to Daryl's family. When they moved in, Alexa, then sixteen, claimed the bedroom the previous owners had added for their daughter.

Sadly, soon after moving to Michigan, Allen was killed in an airplane accident. A few weeks after Allen's passing, Alexa was relaxing in bed when she felt someone take hold of her foot and squeeze. Thinking it was one of their two cats, Alexa tried to shake off the grip, but it didn't work. She could still feel the pressure against her foot, so she sat up, intending to shoo the cat away with her hands, but the cat wasn't there. No one was there, but she could still feel someone holding on to her foot and squeezing.

Alexa fled the room and refused to sleep in it again for at least six weeks. She finally agreed to sleep in there again after Daryl spent the night in her room just to prove to her that it was safe. "Although," he told me, "I admit I kept my feet curled up so they weren't near the edge of the bed."

Daryl and his family believe that if we assume spirits are real, it's possible Allen's death was so sudden and disorienting that his spirit may not have made it to the other side. In his confused state, he might have returned to the room he'd made for his daughter, to say goodbye to her. If that is the case, it seems like Allen must have found the closure he was looking for, because Alexa never felt anyone grab her foot again after that.

That wasn't the end of this family's paranormal experiences, however. A few years later, they had a different kind of eerie experience.

One night Daryl dreamed that he was in his mother's house. In the dream, he descended into the basement, which he'd always thought was haunted, and a grey cloud swooped out of the shadows of a darkened room and wrapped itself around him, enveloping him completely. "My blood turned to ice," he recounted, "and I couldn't move." Eventually, after some struggle, he managed to pull himself free.

As soon as he escaped from the cloud in his dream, he woke up. He was lying in bed, thinking about the dream (and no doubt willing his heartbeat to return to normal), when he heard his daughter's bedroom door open. That familiar sound reassured him that he was in his own home, not his mother's, and everything was as it should be. Every night the family's two cats slept with his daughter, but at some point they would always scratch at the door to be let out — just as was happening now. Feeling better, Daryl eventually managed to fall back asleep.

A couple of days later, Daryl told his wife about his disturbing dream. Jill's face got a little pale, her eyes a little wide, and she asked Daryl if he'd told Alexa about his dream. When he said he hadn't, Jill explained that Alexa had told her that on the night of Daryl's nightmare, the cats hadn't simply meowed and scratched quietly at the door like they normally did. Instead, they were completely freaked out. Their running around, yowling, and jumping on the bed woke

Alexa and she turned over to see a grey cloud hovering over her bed. Alarmed, she turned the light on and the cloud disappeared.

That was when she let the cats out, the sound from which Daryl had drawn so much comfort. If he'd known what was happening on the other side of the door, I wonder if he'd have managed to get back to sleep again that night.

"Here's what I think happened," Daryl said. "A spirit entered our home, and even though I was asleep, I sensed it. It was like hearing a telephone when you're asleep and incorporating it into your dream. Then it left my room and floated through to my daughter's room, frightening the cats."

For me, one of the best parts of this story is that Daryl and Alexa didn't speak to each other about what they experienced; they each, independently, told a third person, Jill. So, as Daryl pointed out to me, there was no way they had influenced each other's stories.

Spooky.

- 30 -

Cassandra — River Valley

Several years ago, there was a Friday the 13th in October. And it was also close to the full moon. Cassandra was then attending the University of Alberta, and she and some of her friends were unable to resist all the clichéd goodness that was tied up in that sort of serendipity. A spooky autumn evening with a big, bright, nearly full moon! What was the best way to experience all that had to offer? With a walk in the river valley, of course.

So, a group of them got together and went for a moonlit walk through the river valley. No doubt they were nervous and giggly, probably trying to scare one another a little bit, but then, Cassandra said, as they were walking by one of the paths near Emily Murphy Park, she started to feel really uneasy. "Not just like, 'oh, I'm making really bad decisions,' but more like we were being watched from the woods.... I kept kind of feeling like, out of the corner of my eye something was moving within the trees, but I never heard anything."

Cassandra's impression was that it was a small child, curious about this group of bigger kids who had invaded their space. She felt as if it was dashing forward to sneak a peek at them and then running away, only to come back a few moments later.

I asked her if she felt like it was pacing them from inside the treeline and she said yes. Although they never actually saw any evidence of anyone watching them from the bushes, she said that it felt as if it followed them for quite a long way.

She told me it wasn't especially menacing, just discomforting, but judging from the way Cassandra recounted this story, I'm not sure that the fact they never saw anything didn't make it even more upsetting for them.

Later, back in her dorm room, Cassandra felt as though she wasn't alone, as if something had followed her home. She tried to shake the feeling off and was successful enough that she managed to fall asleep. Almost. She was in that liminal state between being awake and asleep when she had a very disconcerting dream. A paralysis dream — she felt as though she was awake and aware, but she was completely unable to move.

"It was just this brief moment of this face just coming at me," she said. "It was the face of a younger kid, like ten to thirteen-ish."

The dream scared her a little bit, but she didn't feel as if the presence was menacing her. It was just sort of there. Looming. She felt that the presence was occupying a corner of her room; it had felt wrong to her from the time she came back from the river valley with her friends right up until the next morning.

Did something from the river valley follow Cassandra home that night and, after scaring her as she was falling asleep, leave again? Or did Cassandra and her friends, primed by the nearly full moon and all the superstition around Friday the 13th, work themselves up to turn innocuous events into paranormal ones? Tough to say, but that wasn't Cassandra's only brush with the paranormal, and for her second experience, she was neither primed to be frightened nor was she in anyone else's company.

Cassandra, whose degree is in psychology, was heading to a job interview at Alberta Hospital Edmonton. As she turned onto the road that led to the hospital, she was suddenly overcome with an unwelcome feeling. "It was," she said, "like a tripwire." As soon as she'd turned the corner, she felt an intense feeling of foreboding: not only that she shouldn't be there, but that whatever was there wanted her to leave.

Ghost stories and tales of disconcerting feelings abound about Alberta Hospital Edmonton. Is it because it's a psychiatric facility or is there something paranormal at work here?

"I botched that interview," Cassandra said, "and didn't get the job."

I imagine it would be difficult to perform well in a job interview right after feeling like an invisible something didn't want you anywhere near the prospective place of employment. Perhaps that's actually the silver lining in this story, although it probably didn't feel like it at the time. Because she didn't get the job, Cassandra wouldn't ever have to return to those hospital grounds and face that feeling again.

– 31 –

Premee — Alberta Hospital Edmonton

Speaking of Alberta Hospital Edmonton, Premee also has a story set there.

Back in 2014, she and a friend she was visiting at the hospital went out for a walk. The thing to know about Alberta Hospital Edmonton is that it's not just one building — it is made up of several of them, all spread out across beautifully landscaped grounds, with trees and grass and paths. Anyone I've ever spoken to who has gone to the hospital has remarked upon how amazing the grounds are … but they've also mentioned that there is something unsettling about the place. Perhaps some of that feeling comes from the fact the hospital used to treat people with mental illness. "Mental illness," of course, comes with a stigma, and many feel uncomfortable around those who suffer from it, but perhaps the unsettling feeling that some have experienced at the hospital arises from something else....

Anyway, a couple of years ago, Premee was there visiting a friend, and they were walking around the grounds. Many of the buildings weren't in use at the time. They weren't barricaded or boarded up or anything, but even so, Premee said it was pretty obvious which buildings were in use and which were not. She and her friend were taking their time, walking through the grounds, and Premee was taking lots of pictures of the buildings around them. They stopped in front of Building No. 1, which was clearly not in use. Premee took a handful of photographs and then put her phone away. Just as she was doing so, she saw one of the curtains on the top floor move.

"The movement was so sudden I nearly jumped out of my skin," Premee told me. "I did not see a hand — just a quick flash of white face. It was extremely noticeable because the curtain was also white, so it stood out against the dark window."

"Huh," her friend said. "I thought this one wasn't in use anymore."

Premee felt even more disconcerted, not reassured, that her friend had also seen the face and the movement. The worst part was that the movement of the curtain felt deliberate and timed — as though whoever, or whatever, had moved it had waited until they stopped and were looking in the right direction to see it.

It's definitely possible that the face belonged to a person, but the building was out of use, so there was no easy explanation for why someone would be up on the top floor, looking out at the people walking the grounds. But even if it was a person — say, a caretaker, or a patient who wanted to get away from staff for a while — the experience was very creepy for Premee. In fact, when she went back to visit her friend some weeks later, she insisted that they avoid the entire area around Building No. 1.

"My entire impression of the place," she said, "was 'Wow. This is a really not-good facility to put people with severe mental illness in, maybe.'"

- 32 -

Sandi — Devon

Sandi speaks very quickly. I get the impression that it's necessary, for her to match the speed of her thoughts. In trying to keep up with her, I think that at times I may have looked somewhat distracted. Perhaps that's why I'm not sure she wholly believed me when I said that although I was a skeptic, I was interested in sharing her stories, not debunking them, because more than once she ended a story with, "So explain that." I think I won her over in the end, though.

Sandi lives in Devon, a small town just outside of Edmonton, and some of her stories take place there — okay, I'm bending the rules about stories being set in Edmonton a wee bit — but some, like this first one, take place very firmly within the city limits.

Early one September morning in 1974, Sandi had her first paranormal experience. It took place in her home, just off Whyte Avenue in Edmonton. She was nine years old, and only the day before they'd learned that her favourite cousin, who had lived with them for a time, had died in a car crash.

Everyone was shocked and upset. He'd only been in his early twenties, and everyone felt awful that he'd been taken from them so suddenly.... It was a difficult time. Sandi said she was told to go play in the playroom downstairs. She suspects that the grown-ups just wanted her out of their hair for a little bit.

She was down there, playing by herself, when all of a sudden she saw a white, cloudy shape appear in front of her. Somehow, without knowing how, she came to the understanding that it was her cousin. "I'm okay," he said, and then the cloudy shape dispersed, like smoke in a breeze.

"After that," she told me, "little things would happen that made me feel like he was still there." Sometimes she had a feeling of his presence, or just a sense that she was not alone. Sometimes, if she was looking for something, it would just appear — like he was there, helping her. Looking over her. It was a good feeling, especially since she'd considered him almost like an older brother.

Later, as an adult, Sandi moved into a house in Devon. The town had begun its existence as an intentional community. Planned by Imperial Oil after the company made a huge oil discovery nearby, it was, according to Mrs. V. Hunter, who contributed a piece to the historical section of the Town of Devon's website, "a model town not only in its physical aspects, but even more so in its spirit."

Sandi's house was very small, about eight hundred square feet, and quite old, one of the first ones built by Imperial, being constructed in 1948. When she moved in, the house still had its original structure, fixtures, and features, including an in-floor furnace. It was set in a crawl space in the basement, and there was a big vent in the hallway that you'd have to step over to reach either of the two bedrooms.

As one of the oldest houses in the town, the house definitely had some history. At least two different people had died on the property: one had had cancer and another died accidentally of carbon monoxide poisoning in the garage.

When Sandi, her husband, and her son, then only a few months old, moved in, she threw a wool blanket over the grate so she wouldn't have to keep stepping over it as she was moving things into the house. Finally, exhausted after a long July day of moving and unpacking, Sandi went to sleep. Unfortunately, she didn't get to sleep the night through because in the wee hours of the morning, she was woken by someone shaking her shoulder and saying, "Wake up, wake up, wake up!"

When she woke up, there was no one there, but she immediately knew the problem was the blanket over the furnace vent, so she bolted out of bed and pulled the blanket off the grate. There was a hole burned through the centre of it from the furnace's pilot light.

Whoever, or whatever, had woken Sandi up that night may have prevented a tragedy. If that blanket had been given more time to smoulder and possibly ignite, who knows how the story would have ended.

A few nights later, Sandi's husband was out of town for work; while he was gone, she kept having the same terrifying dream about a cult leader and his crazed followers who lived in her crawlspace basement and were coming to get her. One night, Sandi woke from the dream to find it was storming outside — rain and thunder and lightning. The upset of the storm pretty accurately matched how Sandi was feeling inside. She had had enough.

While the storm raged outside, Sandi grabbed a flashlight and went through the hatch in the floor that led to the basement. She crawled around the whole area in her pyjamas, including going behind the furnace and, basically, covering every inch of the space she possibly could. "I just had to find out what the hell was causing this dream," she said.

She didn't find anything unusual, but after that, the dream never happened again. If nothing else, I think this story says a lot about the power of simply facing our fears and how that can take their power away.

Some months later, Sandi bought a bracelet at a home jewellery party hosted by a friend. That night, it was just her and her young son in the home. They spent a typical evening for them and then they went to bed. The next morning, Sandi woke up and realized her bracelet was no longer on her wrist. She wasn't too concerned about it, though, because she hadn't gone anywhere after her friend's house. She just assumed she'd lost the bracelet in her bedding while she slept. She had plans for that day, so she didn't bother to look for it right away; instead, she just got dressed and went on with her day.

That evening, when it was her son's bedtime, she opened the top drawer of the dresser in his bedroom to get out his pyjamas, and there was her bracelet. All the clothes, and there were a lot of them, had been pushed out of the centre of the drawer, leaving an empty square space, and the bracelet was right in the middle of it. What's more, the clasp was broken off the bracelet and had been placed right in the centre of it.

"I had not been in that drawer that morning," she told me, "because it was his pyjama drawer. So, explain that." Her son was too young to be responsible; he was younger than two at that time — far more likely to stick a broken bracelet in his mouth than to position it perfectly in the centre of a drawer like that.

Frequently, when she was in the living room, Sandi would see the shadow of a man out of the corner of her eye, and for whatever reason she felt like that shadow belonged to the spirit that had taken her bracelet.

Sandi wasn't the only one who spotted the spirit. One day, completely unprompted, the thirteen-year-old babysitter said to her, "I've seen your ghost, you know." When Sandi asked her to elaborate, she said, "He stands in that corner," and pointed to exactly the same corner that Sandi always saw him in. Sandi hadn't mentioned the shadow to anyone outside the family before, certainly not to her babysitter, so she was quite surprised by the revelation. She never felt menaced by the shadow, though, nor did the babysitter, so it got filed away as just "one of those things."

Some months later, Sandi and her husband renovated the house somewhat, tearing out the wall between the living room and the kitchen and replacing it with a shelf so you could see the kitchen from the living room and vice versa. One evening, Sandi, the babysitter, and the babysitter's boyfriend were going to watch a movie, but they could not find the remote control. You know how it is: sure, it's possible to push the buttons manually, but it drives you a little bit bonkers to know there is a remote control somewhere and you just don't know where. So they tore the place apart looking for it. They looked in all the usual places. They looked in unusual places. They looked everywhere they could think of, but with no luck.

Knowing the babysitter knew about the ghost, Sandi jokingly said, "Hey, ghost? Where's that remote control?" Everyone laughed but then they went on with the movie watching, even though they hadn't found the remote. A little while later, Sandi went into the kitchen to get something and looked down to find the remote control sticking out from underneath the fridge.

"Explain that," she said.

When her best friend's father died, Sandi and her friend decided to have a séance to try and contact him.

"We decided to have a séance," Sandi told me, matter-of-factly.

"Okay. In the haunted house," I replied, implying "hey, a séance in the haunted house, what could go wrong?"

Sandi ignored my implication and just agreed. "In the haunted house," she said.

I definitely get the impression that Sandi isn't afraid of much.

So they set up for the séance in the kitchen, including placing candles along the ledge and one in the window. It was wintertime and the window was frosted on the outside, but that same frost just served to amplify the warm light of the flame.

Neither Sandi nor her friend had ever attended a séance before, so they weren't really sure what they were doing. They were just figuring things out as best they could and doing things like holding hands and calling to the friend's dad.

Suddenly, the flame on the candle in the window flared up and then back down. Sandi insisted that it was not a little flicker; the flame suddenly grew at least two feet taller and then shrunk back down to normal. There were no drafts, and no one had suddenly dumped an accelerant on it. The flame just became huge and then small again without any human interaction at all.

"Explain that one."

"Something was there," Sandi said of the house. And other people who visited felt it too, but it was comforting, not menacing. In fact, it made people feel welcome and comfortable in the house.

"Imaginary" friends, on the other hand — possibly not so nice.

When one of Sandi's sons was three, he had an imaginary friend, a unicorn named Corn. This "friend" was never allowed in the house. It wasn't Sandi who said he wasn't allowed in the house; it was her son.

"Well," I said, "I'm with your son; unicorns don't belong in the house."

One day, when her son was trying to close the door, apparently Corn was trying to get inside, and Sandi watched her son struggle with the invisible creature. The way he did it, one foot up pushing against something she couldn't see, fighting to pull the door closed, went beyond the bounds of simple imaginary play. Sandi doesn't know what Corn was, but she is pretty darn sure it wasn't imaginary.

"There was something there," she told me, with no shred of doubt in her mind.

In 2001, Sandi's mother died. When her mother was alive, she was the kind of person who called every day. She didn't need a reason; she just liked to touch base and chat.

Sandi's dad called her early in the morning and said something had happened to her mother and that she should come to their home in Calmar right away. By the time Sandi arrived, her mother had passed — of a heart aneurysm. Much later in the day, when Sandi got back home after spending the day with her father, she was sitting in the living room, just trying to process everything and unwind, when the phone rang. The call display was no help; it just read "Incoming Call," so Sandi answered it and said hello, but there was no response. So she hung up. A couple of minutes later, the phone rang again with that same vague call-display message of "Incoming Call." She answered it and said, "Hello, hello?" but there was no response.

That happened at least half a dozen times before they realized how weird it was that the call display was so vague. Normally, when people called, the phone would show their name and number, but for these phantom phone calls, the display just read, "Incoming Call."

"That's your mom calling," her husband said.

"Yeah, I know," Sandi said.

That happened for the first day and a half after her mother died.

"Did you find that comforting, your mother calling you?" I asked Sandi, because I think I would be stressed beyond belief if our positions were reversed.

Sandi said it was comforting for her because it was fitting. It was in character for her mother.

In the months after her mother died, a few times Sandi had another weird thing happen to her, something I wouldn't mind experiencing myself. She would be minding her own business, standing in her kitchen or, one time, walking through the bingo hall, and a five-dollar bill would float down in front of her from somewhere above her head. At first, she looked for logical explanations — had there been money on the top of the fridge that had been disturbed by a draft, or the air movement caused by her walking into the room? But no, that wasn't the case. She was never able to find a mundane cause for the money that seemed to materialize just above her and then float down in front of her. It happened a handful of different times in all sorts of different locations — her house, the bingo hall, the shopping mall. Weird, but kind of awesome.

Around the time that the money stopped appearing around her, Sandi had a dream that her mother rode a Greyhound bus with all her friends to visit Sandi's house. She came into the house and reassured Sandi that she was fine, and Sandi needn't worry about her anymore, and then she left on the bus and drove away with all her friends. And after that, Sandi never had any further unexplained events connected to her mother.

"I don't know if that was just something, like she went away for real, like she was just moving on, or if I just finally accepted it," Sandi said. Either way, it was a peaceful feeling.

"I like that," I said. "Whether it was a visitation or an acceptance, I like it. It's gentle and happy, and she's not alone. She's on a bus with all her friends.… I mean, I don't know if I'd want to be on the Greyhound for all of eternity, but with friends, maybe."

Not all of Sandi's brushes with the paranormal are connected to her home or her personal life, though; at least once it happened at work. Sandi used to work in housekeeping at a local hospital, and sometimes at lunch time she and some of her co-workers would go to the physiotherapy room and hot-pack themselves as a way of relaxing for an hour before they went back to work. One day, when an older gentleman who was very well known and beloved in the town passed away, Sandi was the first of her friends to reach the physiotherapy room. While she was waiting for them, the radio was on and the station changed. It didn't just change a little bit; it ran from one end of the dial down to the other and then back again.

"That was wrecking my Zen," Sandi told me, so she got up to turn it off, but when she looked at it, something was wrong. Not only was the radio not turned on, it wasn't even plugged in. When her colleagues showed up a short time later, she told them about it and they just shrugged and said, "Yeah, there's lots of ghosts here."

"And there were," Sandi said. "There were lots of ghosts. We'd see weird people in the laundry area and stuff."

She told me this casually, as if such a thing was commonplace. The same way I might say, "I had chai with my breakfast today." The fact that she said it like it wasn't really a thing struck me. It might be no big deal for her, but I wanted to know more.

"Tell me about the weird people in the laundry area," I said.

While she and some of her co-workers were working in the laundry room, they would sense they weren't alone. They could feel the presence of someone, or something, else. And they'd see them too, or glimpses of them. There'd be a flicker of movement, or a figure. Once, Sandi saw an old lady in a nightgown; another time, someone completely different.

"I'm so glad you saw my Facebook post," I said as our conversation drew to a close.

"Yeah?" Sandi said. "And it's all gospel truth."

"These are good stories. I'm going to have fun writing them," I said.

"And the weird thing is, six years ago I was diagnosed with cancer and I was given six months to live. But I'm still here and I'm all good, and I haven't had any weird experiences since I had my chemo and my surgery. It's like they took that part out of me."

Despite not recently having had any weird experiences, Sandi did have one last story about something that happened not that long ago. She had rented the old Imperial Oil building in Devon. It had been empty for quite a long time and at some point in that period it had been flooded, so there was superficial damage and water stains all over, and the ceiling was disgusting. While she was cleaning it up, Sandi kept feeling uncomfortable. She didn't know of any specific event or incident to point to as a reason for it, so she asked a couple of local metaphysical experts to come, take a look, and see if the space would benefit from being smudged.

When they (Sandi, her husband, and the two experts) arrived, they couldn't get the door open. Sandi unlocked it, but when they tried to pull it open, it just would not budge. She recalled the two women looking at one another with wide eyes and saying, "It does not want us here."

They surrendered the battle of the door to whatever was keeping it closed, and instead went around to the other door, which opened without any difficulty. The women walked from room to room and then used sage to cleanse it. Once they'd cleansed the entire building, they told Sandi that down in the boiler room, they had sensed some sort of ancient entity. They described him as being a grey-green mass who wasn't going to hurt anyone, but he was very angry. He wasn't attached to the room — he was attached to the land. They thought perhaps he was angry because the building was associated with petroleum, which, if he was a nature spirit associated with the land, might be anathema to him. The women suggested that, to appease him, Sandi might want to plant a tree or some other sort of plant.

After they'd finished doing their cleansing, the air in the building felt a thousand times lighter than before, Sandi said.

– 33 –

Fraser — Gateway Boulevard

Fraser's story involves a business, not a home, but I've put it in this section because I wasn't able to find enough about the history of the building to warrant including it alongside other locations for which I could get full histories. Still, I wanted to include it somewhere because his stories are fabulous and definitely hair-raising.

The building, which currently houses F2 Furnishings on Gateway Boulevard, was once a movie theatre. In fact, even though the main level has become a furniture showroom, it is my understanding that the theatre projection area still exists, largely intact. Back when it was a Famous Players/Empire Theatres movie theatre, Fraser used to work there.

Although not the case now, historically, being a movie projectionist was a very dangerous job. The film that movies were recorded on — celluloid — is ridiculously dangerous. I think the website Atlas Obscura describes it wonderfully.

> Celluloid is … extremely dangerous. It is essentially a solid form of nitroglycerin dragged across super-hot carbon rods at extremely high speed. If celluloid combusts, which it can do at "car parked in the sun" temperatures, the fire generates its own oxygen,

creating a flame that cannot be extinguished. It can burn underwater. It can burn beneath a fire blanket. It burns until the celluloid is gone, and any attempt to smother it creates clouds of poison gas.*

Because of the dangers of celluloid, projection rooms were set away from audiences and had myriad security measures in place to prevent catastrophe — measures that sometimes included sealing the room off completely (whether the projectionist was still in there or not). When Rona, my family, and I toured the Garneau Theatre, I asked the projectionist about what, if any, safety measures — such as fire shutters or oxygen-consuming fire suppression systems — the theatre had sported back in the day. He dodged my question with a joke, and I let things pass. I really would have liked to know, though; in all sincerity, that sort of thing has always captured my imagination because of all the horrifying "what if?" possibilities.

When Fraser worked at the theatre on Gateway Boulevard, all the whispered workplace rumours about ghosts didn't involve a fire; however, they did involve the projection booth. Legend was that in the projection area, an old projectionist had died of heat exhaustion and his ghost continued to haunt the building.

Fraser actually remembers being up in the projection area and hearing footsteps he couldn't explain. He would sometimes hear footsteps in the projection booth when he was alone in the room, or sometimes when he and a single colleague were in there together. On every occasion, neither Fraser nor his co-worker were moving, and yet they could hear someone, or something, walking around the room.

Although he never saw anything himself, Fraser heard stories from some of his co-workers who claimed to have actually seen the apparition of a little girl all by herself in Theatre 6. Some also said that they had witnessed sinks turning on without any human intervention.

* atlasobscura.com/articles/the-explosive-truth-behind-the-movie-theater-projection-room

The most frightening thing Fraser experienced in the theatre happened when he was alone in the building with his manager. Everyone else had left for the night and the doors were all locked up tight. Fraser and his manager were in a back office, counting money. They were each in different spaces, separated only by a glass wall. All of a sudden, it sounded as though someone was knocking loudly on the glass. Four times they heard the noise, and then, in Fraser's words, "We booked it the heck outta there!"

– 34 –

Mike — Castle Downs and Gariepy

Mike told me that he's lived in two different haunted houses with spirits of two very different personality types. At the first house, a bi-level situated in Castle Downs, Mike said he had the very distinct impression that something didn't want him there. The energy of the house felt very negative, unwelcoming, and, at times, even menacing. And not just toward him. Mike's dad once heard a demonic-sounding growl coming from the basement, startling him so much that he jumped out of bed. For a week afterward, he absolutely refused to go down into the basement — his fear was that strong.

Mike's sleep was also disturbed in the home. On more than one occasion, he was wakened in the wee hours of the morning by voices. The voices would continue until he got up and checked to make sure there wasn't a television or radio on somewhere, and then they would fall silent. He never felt threatened by whomever or whatever those voices belonged to; mostly, he just felt annoyed, and would immediately go back to sleep once the voices stopped. Much more menacing were the times he woke in the middle of the night and felt something heavy pressing down on him. It felt exactly like a physical presence, but whatever it was, it was invisible. Invisible, but strong. Strong enough to hold him in place.

These sorts of encounters often resulted in Mike feeling ill the next day — a consequence, he believes, of the entity, whatever it was, feeding off his energy. One of the reasons he thinks this is because when a family member became seriously ill (it should be noted that Mike doesn't actually think the illness was caused by anything other-worldly), the paranormal activity that affected Mike tapered off. He believes this might be because the entity was feeding off his family member's energy at that time, instead of his. Once that family member passed on, things started happening to Mike again. It was as if, he thinks, the being had taken everything it could from Mike's family member and now was turning its attention back to him.

Shortly after the paranormal activity picked up again, Mike actually saw the entity he believes was haunting his house. He was brushing his teeth one evening when, in the mirror, he saw a man walking down the hallway. It wasn't a member of Mike's family; this man was dressed in a tuxedo and wearing a top hat and, perhaps most tellingly, he was semi-transparent. Mike later spotted the same man walking in the opposite direction down the same hallway. This second time he saw him, it was broad daylight. Did the spirit spend his time pacing up and down the hallway? To me, that does not sound like a fun way to spend eternity.

Possibly even creepier, a couple of days after Mike first spotted the man in the top hat, he saw a shadowy head just outside his window. Under some circumstances, that might be considered a bit unusual, but not especially creepy. However, Mike's window was very high up. As he put it, any man would have to be "inhumanly" tall to have his head line up with the window.

Finally, in what could easily be a scene out of a horror movie, Mike said one time he was just lying in bed, when suddenly he felt one end of the bed lift off the ground, with him in it. It didn't stay up in the air for very long, but he definitely had an impression of being weightless for a few moments.

Mike said that when he was in the house, he felt like he was constantly surrounded by a negative energy, as if there was something there that wanted him to leave. He thinks that he and his family's Christian faith kept them safe from the being, and that perhaps their prayers sapped some of its powers.

Eventually, he and his family moved from that home (for reasons unrelated to the haunting), but the last time he was in it, Mike had a feeling like the spirit that haunted it wasn't through with him. It seemed to Mike that the spirit was certain they'd meet again. He told me that he felt as though the entity was saying, "I don't want you here, but we have unfinished business."

The second haunted house that Mike lived in was in the Gariepy neighbourhood. The spirit in this house seemed to be of a character totally different from the one in his Castle Downs home. This spirit wasn't threatening at all; in fact, Mike describes most of its activities as "antics," which makes them sound like the sort of thing a playful or mischievous child might indulge in. Mike says the ghost would move things around, and cause phantom smells. One time he noticed the smell of burnt toast. This was unusual, not only because no one had made (or burned) any toast recently, but also because the smell didn't stay in one place. It was highly concentrated in one area, but that area kept moving around — like a little cloud, or a person. It did a loop from the back door, though the kitchen, into the living room and then into the foyer, before eventually fading away as it went up the stairs to the second level.

On two different occasions, the spirit decided to mess with Mike and one of his friends while they were hanging out in the basement. They were sitting on the couch, doing nothing in particular, when they both happened to look over and see the DVD case for *Spiderman 3* slowly lift off an end table and hover in the air. Shocked, Mike reached over and slammed it back down onto the table where it belonged. He and his friend weren't afraid, though, and both seemed to accept that what had just occurred was weird, but not really worth freaking out about.

A short time later, he and his friend were playing a video game. Things were not going well in the game, and the two of them were raging (cursing and shouting) at the game. Then, just behind them, they heard an old man's voice say, "Language." It was a stern warning from an older man. When they looked to see who had spoken, however, there was nobody there.

On a different occasion, when Mike and a friend were playing video games in the basement — being very careful of their language, I'm sure — they both felt a cold wind rush past them. It was dramatic enough that they paused the game to see if they could track down an open vent or door that might be letting in a draft. They couldn't. Besides, it was a nice summer day, so it didn't seem possible that there would be a wayward cold breeze. Was the ghost just making his presence known again?

When Mike eventually moved from that house, he felt like the spirit was saddened by his going, exactly the opposite of how he'd felt leaving the previous house.

Over the course of researching this book, I have spoken to several people who've told me they didn't live in a haunted home but felt that they themselves might be haunted. When Mike first started telling me his story, I wondered if he was going to head in that direction as well, as he's had so many unexplained encounters, but he did not. Perhaps because the character of the two main entities he encountered were so different? I wonder if he has so many stories because he's very open to the idea of a spirit world and paranormal phenomena? Rona frequently tells me ghosts can't be bothered to reveal themselves to unbelievers. Assuming that the opposite is true — they are more likely to reveal themselves to people who aren't skeptical about their existence — helps to explain why Mike has experienced more than most people.

Like so many things that fall into the paranormal realm, we'll probably never know for sure.

– 35 –

Tanya — Parkallen

Comparing notes some years later, Tanya and her brother discovered that when they were children they both, independently, believed that one of the upstairs bedrooms of their childhood home was a portal to somewhere evil. Her brother is eleven years older than her, and because they didn't have a particularly close relationship when they were younger, they never talked about it back then. It was only later, as adults, that they discovered they'd each come to the same conclusion about that door, even though neither one of them could pinpoint exactly why they had.

When they asked their mother about it, she said, "Oh, no, no, no …" but the portal, or non-portal as the case may be, was far from the only eerie thing about their home.

Tanya — the same Tanya who shared her stories about Scona Pool and Queen E school — grew up surrounded by spirits. Her mother never doubted their existence and would interact with them and speak about them to her children the same way she would any living beings. There is, as I've said before, not a drop of skepticism in Tanya or her mother, and that's reflected in the stories she tells and the fact that spirits are just there, in the background of life, all the time. And they always have been.

When Tanya was younger, they lived in a single-family house that had been converted into a multi-family home. At first the family lived upstairs and rented the lower level, and then later they moved downstairs and rented the upstairs to her aunt.

Tanya hated going from the upstairs to the downstairs. "I could come down those thirteen steps in about two seconds, and I had it worked that I would throw open the door with the right hand, shut off the lights with the left hand, and slam the door in about a second without even looking back."

Tanya's mother noticed this behaviour and asked her what was inspiring it. "What is it," her mother asked, "that you're trying not to see?"

Tanya didn't even hesitate before answering, "A tall, thin man, and a heavy woman."

The spirits weren't angry or menacing, but Tanya just didn't like seeing them. And they were frequently there: that was their space.

They weren't the only spirits Tanya grew up sharing a space with.

One evening when Tanya was alone in the house, she was sitting in the living room. From that room she could see into the kitchen; she saw the ghost of her maternal grandfather, whom she didn't remember because he'd died when she was two. Her grandfather wasn't alone; her uncle, who was also deceased, was there with him. When her parents and her aunt came home, she said, "Opa and Uncle Charlie were here."

Her mother and her aunt quizzed her on who she'd seen and she described them perfectly, mentioning details that can't be captured in a photograph, like exactly how someone stands, or moves, or smokes a pipe. She nailed all the details. Her aunt paled at how precise Tanya's description was, but her mother was happy for her. "Oh, how nice, Tanya," she said (she said this a lot).

For a time, Tanya's brother's room was in the back sunroom. The sunroom was a later addition, built over a dirt cellar that had a coal chute, the doors of which were in that room. Once, before Tanya was even born, or at best when she was very small, her brother was using a flashlight to read in bed past his bedtime. The family cat started to become agitated, and was even growling deep in her throat. Then she jumped off the bed, went underneath it, and began to fight with something. The fight went on for a couple of minutes. Tanya's brother decided that he was certainly not going to stick any part of his body over the edge of the bed, not even to look at what was going on. Finally, the cat came up, looking a bit worse for wear. She climbed under the sheets and went to sleep.

"That's not okay," I said when Tanya told me this story.

"But then he told my mother, and she just said, 'It's okay, dear, don't worry about it.'"

Speaking of Tanya's brother. You know how words of wisdom are often passed between children in a family, especially from older siblings to younger ones? Tanya has never forgotten one of the bits of advice that her brother gave her: "Do not sit by the heat registers, because those vents are how *they* travel."

He was never specific about who or what *they* were, but it was clear that one didn't want to cross paths with them or attract their attention.

In many families, one might pass this off as a bit of mischief, an older brother teasing his little sister, but in Tanya's family, where spirits were just an accepted fact, it seems like perhaps it was more than that. And Tanya never once considered that he might be joking or pulling her leg. Not once.

Stay away from the air vents. That's how they travel.

Isn't that beautifully creepy? I bet you'll never think of the weird noises your furnace makes in the same way again. I know I won't.

It wasn't just family members who experienced the spirits that hung about Tanya's childhood home, either. One time she had a friend over and they were up in her aunt's kitchen, baking cookies, when they heard someone open the front door, walk through the house, and go out the back door. Tanya remembers her friend looking over at her in confusion and saying, "What was that?"

Tanya said it was the front door, and her friend pointed out that their front door wasn't functional. In fact, it was taped closed to keep any drafts coming through it.

"Oh, I know," Tanya explained. "But that's my Uncle Charlie."

"How are you so calm about this?" her friend asked, and Tanya replied, "Because it is. It just is."

Things are the way they are, and Tanya doesn't get worked up about them.

She and her friend went downstairs to investigate and found the front door closed, the tape around the edges intact. What's more, the back door was also still secured, including a bolt along the bottom that could only be closed from the inside, so no one could go through it and then lock that behind them. And yet, both girls had distinctly heard the sound of someone coming in the front door, walking through the house, and then going out the back door.

After her father died, Tanya's family sold the house. The first step in doing that was to empty it out, including the basement that Tanya had never liked going into the whole time she'd lived there. To expedite the process, she and her friends formed a human chain and passed things up from the basement and into the yard, to be sorted and dealt with.

When Tanya was in the dirt cellar beneath her brother's room, she'd cleared the bulk of stuff out and was going through the miscellanea that was left behind, somewhat buried in the dirt floor. Tanya found a horseshoe and looked at her friend who was a few feet away and said, "I want to keep this," and her friend said, "Okay."

Then, Tanya put her hand back in the dirt and looked over at her friend. Her friend's face was no longer happy and relaxed, but drawn and concerned. "We need to get out now," her friend said, and Tanya agreed. "Yeah," she said. "We need to get out now."

They just knew, suddenly, that they weren't welcome there anymore, and they didn't feel safe there anymore, either.

Was this the same thing the family cat had fought with all those years ago? Keeping it contained to the dirt cellar beneath her brother's old room?

When Tanya told her mother about this, her mother, who usually responds to reports of ghosts and haunting with, "Oh, how nice Tanya," said, "Oh. I'd wondered if that was still there."

Not he. Not she. That.

Her mother never expounded on what she thought might be down there, perhaps because Tanya was upset. She'd told her mother before that she felt like there was something scary in the basement and her mother had always brushed her concerns aside. Now, when Tanya was an adult, her mother was confirming that actually, there had been something concerning down there after all. The whole time.

"Why didn't you tell me?" Tanya asked.

"Well," her mother said, "if I had, would you ever have gone down there and done your own laundry?"

A very practical lady, Tanya's mother is. I'm a pretty big fan of hers.

Moving forward from there, anytime Tanya's mother told her there weren't any spirits in a given location, Tanya would say, "Okay. Is this, like, for real there's nothing there, or is this like 'I want you to do your own laundry' there's nothing there?" A legitimate question, it seems to me, under the circumstances.

Later, Tanya moved into a house on the same block, with two roommates. A house that was owned by her parents and that they used to rent out for extra income. That house was also haunted.

One incident involved her first roommate, whom we'll call Heidi, coming in and seeing the second roommate, Brandon (not his real name), sitting on the sofa in the living room. She greeted him and then continued on through to the kitchen. He didn't respond so she went back to see what was up, but there wasn't anyone there. She didn't think much about it until a short time later, when Brandon came in the front door.

"I thought you were already here," she said, "sitting on the couch."

"Nope," said Brandon. "I just got home."

Heidi was pretty wigged out, so when Tanya came home, she told her all about it. Tanya immediately called her mother to find out what the deal was. Or, as Tanya put it, she called and said, "Okay, so who's the guy?"

After Tanya described the man to her mother, her mother said, "Oh, that must be one of the brothers."

"Oh, so he's okay?" Tanya asked.

"Oh yeah, he's fine, Tanya," her mother replied.

So, Tanya was like, okay, good, fine. Everything's normal. "Because," she told me, "if my mom says no, that's when we all panic. Unless, of course, she's lying again."

It seems that brothers and a sister had lived in the house some years before. One of the men had an intellectual disability and the other had severe diabetes. Tanya has sensed the brother with the intellectual disability just sort of lingering, or in one case walking behind her down the hall. He is anything but menacing.

When he was alive, he used to come and get Tanya's mother anytime his brother was in medical distress. Because the brother's diabetes was not well controlled, that happened not infrequently. Sadly, the older, diabetic brother actually died in the house, in Tanya's kitchen.

For a time, Tanya kept waking up in the wee hours of the morning and feeling a masculine presence in the room with her. It wasn't scary, just discomforting, because he didn't really belong there. When she consulted with her mother about it, her mother hypothesized that perhaps it was the younger brother. Maybe he had passed now and was coming back to the last place he'd seen his brother, looking for him.

On her mother's advice, before Tanya went to bed that night, she told the spirit that he could move on, that his brother — and probably his sister — were waiting for him. "And also," her mother said, "tell him I said hi."

Have I mentioned that to Tanya and her mother, ghostly friends are just like any other friends?

Anyway, Tanya relayed all the messages, and after that she was no longer woken by someone unseen in her bedroom. Still, often when she comes into the house, she can hear voices talking to one another. It's as if she's left a radio on, except that a few seconds after she comes in the door, the voices will stop. Sort of like how if you walk into a room and people are talking about you, it will suddenly fall silent. Exactly like that. Tanya doesn't know who the voices belong to, but she thinks that perhaps they are the voices of the siblings who used to live there.

Why does Tanya have so many paranormal encounters, and other people, people like me, do not? I asked her and she said, "I think everybody has the ability [to sense spirits], but do they draw on it? Do they welcome spirits?"

That sounds like the sort of answer Rona would also give. You have to be open to them for them to be open to you. If you totally don't believe in them, why should they waste their time with you?

On the one hand, the argumentative part of me wants to say, "Well, they have nothing but time, right?" but then another part whispers, "You know how you feel about dealing with people who waste your time." And I'm like, *Yeah … yeah. I kind of get it.*

– 36 –

Ghost Cats

For the last stories in this book, I'd like to talk about ghost cats. In researching paranormal activity, I've discovered that stories about ghost cats seem to come up not infrequently. I was a little surprised at how ghost-cat stories outnumber dog stories, but they really do. Honestly, I'm more of a dog person than a cat person, but I love both of them, so stories about the little furballs persisting after death make my heart happy. It seems to me that including some of them is the perfect way to end this book.

I have two ghost-cat stories to share. Both take place in Edmonton, but involve different people.

Joan's story is interesting because she doesn't think the ghost cat she encountered was her own. (Please note this is not the same Joan I spoke to at Walterdale.)

Some years ago, Joan and two of her friends decided to celebrate the Celtic harvest festival known as *Sauin* (or *Samhain*) by talking about their pets who had passed. The idea was to remember their pets, the joy they'd brought in life, and how much they'd loved them. They thought it would be easier to get close to the spirits of their dearly departed pets, as those who celebrate Sauin believe that on that night, the veil between the worlds of the living and the dead is thin, making it easy for spirits to visit.

The women all met at Joan's house and each of them took turns talking about their pets. One of the women spoke in depth about her big cat, whom she'd loved dearly, and how devastated she'd been when he passed, in part because he'd gone missing shortly before that.

Once the formal part of the celebration was done, they wrapped up with a little wine and snacks and then went their own way.

Two nights later, Joan was woken abruptly from sleep with the distinct feeling that there was a frenzied cat running around and around her room. "It was frantic," she told me, "as if it had been lost but had just been found."

Not satisfied with circling the bed, the beastie jumped up onto it, clawed up Joan's body as if she was a horizontal tree, then sat on her chest and disappeared.

"I think that what happens," Joan said, "is if you have an open connection, if you're kind of a spiritual person yourself, things, people, pets, can be drawn to you. And if they are trying to find themselves out of an earthbound or fear state, they go toward things that are comforting. So, I think maybe that's what happened. This cat finally found its way home and then used me as a door and ran through me to the other place."

The second ghost-cat story is about Sarah's cat, Cynthia. The cat had been only six months old when she came to live with Sarah, but those six months were very trying. Cynthia had originally lived with a low-level drug dealer, and had, it seemed, been fed drugs during that time. So, she had a fair number of issues, including, not surprisingly, trust issues. But even so, she still bonded with Sarah immediately and became "her" cat.

Cynthia lived until she was seventeen. In her later years, she developed a brain tumour, which caused her to go blind. Not being able to see didn't stop Cynthia from meeting Sarah when she came home from work. The cat would hear and recognize Sarah's car and would stop whatever she was doing and go to meet her. On one notable occasion, Cynthia climbed out the second-floor window, down the balcony pillar, and across the street to meet Sarah. All without being able to see.

Perhaps some of this fearlessness came from the fact that Sarah was very patient and encouraging of Cynthia. When she first became blind, Cynthia was sometimes afraid to walk somewhere, unsure if it was safe. Sarah would say, "It's okay, Cynthia, go on."

When Cynthia got really sick, when she was about sixteen, Sarah relented on her "no cats on the bed" rule and allowed Cynthia to join her in bed. "For the last year of her life," Sarah said, "she slept on the bed, on my hip. If I wanted to turn over, I had to wake up, lift the cat, turn over, and put the cat back down before she fully woke up; otherwise, she'd walk around, making me soft again."

I could hear the love in Sarah's voice when she talked about Cynthia, and about their relationship.

Cynthia died peacefully at seventeen. Sarah found her — still warm, waiting at the door. She figured Cynthia had heard her arrive home from work, gotten up from her usual place under the table, come to the door to meet her, and then just died suddenly of a stroke or something of that sort.

The night Cynthia died, Sarah was almost asleep — in that liminal state between dreams and wakefulness — and she heard Cynthia meow. Still in that half-asleep state, Sarah answered automatically, "It's okay, Cynthia, go on."

Almost immediately after the words left her lips, Sarah became fully awake and thought, "What was I saying? I want her to stay!"

It's possible Cynthia did stay at least a while longer, because one of Sarah's friends who was staying at the house frequently felt a cat brush up against her leg, but when she looked, there was no cat.

"Cynthia loved laps," Sarah told me, "but only on her own terms. So she would brush by your legs, and if you let her, she would climb up in your lap and stick her butt in your face and be happy as can be."

In the days after Cynthia's passing, Sarah also occasionally saw a flicker of movement out of the corner of her eye, a movement she attributed to Cynthia. "We always sort of felt that Cynthia had stuck around for a while and was keeping us company in the same old way."

And that is the perfect story to end on.

In Conclusion

When I originally conceived of this book idea and pitched it, first to Rona and then to the publisher, I imagined something quite different from what it's become in the end. I thought I'd be the Scully to Rona's Mulder, not exactly debunking the paranormal activity we saw or that others told us about, but definitely being the skeptic and making that very much a big part of the conversation. You can see the evidence of that initial approach in lots of little ways — how this book is laid out, for example, with the "What We Knew Going In" sections, or how I mention my skepticism right in the first chapter. But as this project moved from idea into reality, things changed; they evolved. Somehow, between when we started out and now, as I write these last few words, my skepticism went from something that needed to be front and centre to almost unimportant, a kind of pro-forma disclaimer that I'd mention as an aside to people before I interviewed them about their eerie encounters. It stopped mattering to me, and my priority became collecting the stories, getting the details right, and sharing them with other people who really like a good ghost story. Story over skepticism every time. The result is a book different from the one I'd first intended to write, but it's a good book. Filled with good stories.

There are some gaps, of course. There are plenty of haunted locations around Edmonton that didn't make it into this book — for a variety of reasons — but I feel like we hit most of the big ones. This book provides, if not a complete compendium of Edmonton ghost stories (which, realistically speaking, could never be compiled), then a very solid starting point. A place to begin to learn about the spooks and haunts of our beautiful city.

And the thing about ghost stories is that they don't need to be contained in a book in order to be shared or spread. As I said way back at the very beginning, everyone has a story. These are just some of them.

Acknowledgements

Rona's Acknowledgements

I need to thank so many people for finally getting me thrust into the publishing world. First of all, thanks to my wonderfully geeky, intelligent writing partner, Rhonda Parrish. You are a great listener (especially with beer and food) and you never failed to show enthusiasm and give me the benefit of the doubt when I would tell you what I was "seeing" and sensing in different places.

Thanks to Dundurn Press for wanting to publish a book on Edmonton and its haunted places.

Thanks to my son, Brett Myckan, and my sister, Corey Anderson; you both are a source of love, humour, and wonderment. I love it when you get excited when you find something paranormal on your cameras and phones; it literally fills me with joy.

A big thanks to my stepdaughters, Dana Myckan, Jodi Myckan, and Kari Myckan; step-granddaughters, Chloe McKort, and Zevan and Keira Whitbeck; and mother-in-law, Stephania Myckan, for being part of my supportive family unit. There are other family members/steps/in-laws too numerous to mention (you know who you are) whom I deeply appreciate for having been there over the years.

Thanks to my very close group of friends: Laurie and Rob Ledrew, Joyce Maycher, Joe Kozak, Ed Fong, Terry and Sabina McLachlan, and Rebecca and Jeremy Reid. You've witnessed my spiritual growth over the years and have put up with all my paranormal recitations without rolling your eyes!

Thanks to the Edmonton Bone-Wagon Association and Robb Eggertson, who helped me acquire my first hearse so I could drive around Edmonton in style!

Thanks to Darryl Plunkie for helping me with the Paranormal Explorers website (and being a partner for many years in scaring people in October), where I post stories about Edmonton and other places. Working on the site has triggered a particular interest in Edmonton and its great haunts, and has really inspired me to get stories about them out there to others.

Thanks to a couple of keen skeptics who have counterbalanced me: my friend Troy Gehmlich, and my step-brother Dave Marcotte. You always need skeptics in your life, even if they don't believe in what you believe in.

Thanks to my mother, Shirle Chambers, who literally forced me to come to live in Edmonton during my eighteenth year of life. I never thought then that it would feel like home, but I have an incredibly strong bond with this city and am fiercely proud of it — with all its beauty and flaws. I know my mother is not physically here anymore, having passed away years ago, but she's around quite a bit, even if I can't always see her. I miss her every day.

A huge thank you to my husband, Ben, who started Paranormal Explorers with me and who's been present through every painful up and down we've had to go through, and all the amazing experiences we've shared over the last thirty-six years. There's no one else who could have put up with me like you have. Love you.

And finally, a warm thanks to all the friends and family who have departed from this dimension but are lodged firmly in my heart and are among us in spirit form. I love and miss you all. But you know that.

Rhonda's Acknowledgements

First and foremost, I would like to thank Rona, without whom this book would not exist. I've appreciated your patience in dealing with my never-ending questions. I loved listening to your stories, and the wit and humour with which you shared them. I hope I have done them justice in the way I've retold them in these pages. Should anyone find fault with their entertainment value, the blame should be on the teller, not the source. I'd go on a ghost-hunting field trip with you any day of the week (just not before noon, okay? ;)).

I would also like to thank all of the other people who shared their stories with me. Some of their stories didn't make it into the book, but I enjoyed hearing every single one. I'm terrified to list names for fear I will leave someone out, but let's give it a shot. Thank you, Val, Eileen, Doug, Sandi, Tanya, Chadwick, Brittney, Daryl, Janice, Chloe, Mike, Fraser, Corinne, Premee, Joan, Other Joan, Sarah, Geri, Jocelyn, and Cassandra. You were all a lot of fun to talk with, every one of you, and I hope you're happy with how I've retold your stories.

In addition, the archivists at the Provincial Archives of Alberta were fantastic. Karen and Alyssa were particularly wonderful, either pointing me in the direction of super-helpful resources or giving me information that was pivotal to the writing of this book.

Everyone at Dundurn has been amazing, especially my favourite mole, erm, developmental editor, Dominic. I really appreciate you making the process painless and the product better.

I know I should have said "book" there, but process, painless, product … how could I pass that alliterative opportunity up?

Finally, my greatest thanks, as always, go to Jo. Your support and general awesomeness make it possible to do this thing I so desperately love to do. Thank you, Jo.

Sources and Further Reading

I consulted a great many sources while I was working on this book. Most of them were people. This was perfect for me, because it meant I could ask questions and get clarity when I wasn't sure about something. It's less awesome for anyone who would like to dig deeper into these stories because, for obvious reasons, I can't just give out those people's contact information. But all is not lost, because I did consult several other resources as well.

canadashistory.ca

Much like the history and archive websites I've listed that are specific to Edmonton, this webpage is filled with photographs, news stories, and archived information. Only, instead of being about one city, it contains stories from our entire country. I mostly consulted it when I was writing about the Charles Camsell Hospital, but it has an amazing selection of stories about our history.

citymuseumedmonton.ca

The Edmonton City as Museum Project website is all about the people, places, and things that make Edmonton … well, Edmonton. The stories are written by a multitude of people, so you get a variety of voices and perspectives.

dundurn.com/books/haunted-hospitals

Mark Leslie and I collaborated on *Haunted Hospitals* a couple of years ago. Not only does it have stories of haunted locations all across Canada and the world, but there is an entire section dedicated to the psychiatric hospital in Ponoka, which is very close to Edmonton. If you like the ghost stories within this book, you'll probably enjoy those in *Haunted Hospitals* as well.

facebook.com/EerieEdmonton

Rona and I have a Facebook page where we're planning to share news about this book as well as other updates about paranormal happenings and haunted locations in and around Edmonton.

paranormalexplorers.com

The primary source for this book was Rona Anderson. She has a website that contains contact information (so you can get in touch with her directly). It also has notes about haunted locations around Edmonton and elsewhere, and stories of some of her investigations at those locations. Some of the stories will be familiar to you, but we couldn't fit all of Rona's stories in this book — not even close.

peel.library.ualberta.ca/newspapers

Peel's Prairie Provinces is a rabbit hole that I frequently lost whole days to, so proceed with caution! They have scans of entire newspapers going as far back as 1871. You may go in thinking that you're just going to look up this one story, then not look away from your monitor again until hours later. Or perhaps that's just me. Either way, this stuff is fascinating.

provincialarchives.alberta.ca

The Provincial Archives of Alberta were invaluable to me as I was working on this book, in particular while researching bits and pieces of the city's history. More than once the archivist on the other side of the "Ask an Archivist" button was able to point me in the right direction or introduce me to resources I might otherwise not have found.

seeksghosts.blogspot.com

This website is filled with a huge selection of ghost stories. For this book, I largely consulted it in regard to the story of Felicia Graham, but in my free time I occasionally flipped through to read ghost stories from places outside of Edmonton.

Image Credits